Cristina Ismael

THE HEALING ENVIRONMENT

THE HEALING ENVIRONMENT

Neither the author nor the publisher make any claims, direct or implied, for any procedures mentioned in this book. No allegations as to the therapeutic properties of any of these procedures are made or intended.

THE HEALING ENVIRONMENT

Cristina Ismael

CELESTIAL ARTS
Millbrae, California

DEDICATION

To the women and men everywhere who will make the healing environment a reality

for Stephanie, whose love knows why

and my mother, who remembers a better world even as I dream of a new one.

Copyright ©1973, 1976 by Cristina Ismael

Photography by Dean Roubos

Published by CELESTIAL ARTS
231 Adrian Road
Millbrae, California 94030

First Printing, September 1976
Made in the United States of America

Library of Congress Cataloging in Publication Data

Ismael, Cristina.
   The healing environment.

   Bibliography: p.
   Includes index.
   1. Mental healing. I. Title.
RZ400.I85   615'.851   75-28758
ISBN: 0-89087-021-7

1 2 3 4 5 6 7 – 82 81 80 79 78 77 76

CONTENTS

Contents

ACKNOWLEDGMENTS

The research for and writing of *The Healing Environment* has taken several years. As with any work such as this, there are those who have helped along the way, for a major enterprise is seldom accomplished singly. In this beautiful and invisible pattern which is the life journey, different people have emerged at various times, giving, in some way, exactly what I needed to go on. There are many I cannot name, who simply spoke to me and expressed their appreciation of the work, reminding me of the need for the healing environment, and giving me energy to go on when my vision was clouded or my faith waning. I wish to express my special appreciation to:

Bonnie Werts, friend and teacher who guided me through the beginning, dreamed with me and asked questions, shared visions, and made publication of the original work possible

Paul Molinari, for the gift of a retreat on his beautiful land where so many of my thoughts on the healing environment were inspired

Gordon Tappan and Norma Lyman, for guidance and counsel during my research

David Van Nuys, for his friendship, knowledge of hypnosis, and wonderful enthusiasm

Janet Cole and Miriam Ginden, for loving help with a simple task that expanded communication

Urmas Kaldveer, for the gift of his books and support

Claude Steiner, for his very fine book, *Scripts People Live,* and the solution it offers to the pronoun quandry. In this book I am interchanging the masculine/feminine pronoun and adjective at random, since all the situations described can be equally applied to either sex. I gratefully acknowledge, and salute, Mister Steiner's precedent in this realm of living language.

8

Dean Roubos, for his unique talent of capturing with the camera those intimate moments of wonder and awe at the natural world. It is a privilege to have his work, which I have always loved and respected, as a part of *The Healing Environment.*

Joycelyn Moulton, my editor, for her tenacity and faith

Susan Nichols, Joseph Hughes, and Mary Harris, for listening, giving, and counseling so clearly during difficult periods of decision

Alberto Villoldo, for paving the way to publication

Anais Nin, for the inspiration and instruction I received from her work, and for the personal support she gave which served as the impetus to turn the original work into a book and

Stephanie Fieri, who has seen me through every phase of the work, and whose help has been inestimable.

Thank you,
Cristina Ismael

PART ONE

ORIGINS

"The old Lakota was wise.
He knew that man's heart
away from nature becomes hard;
he knew that lack of respect
for growing, living things
soon led to lack of respect
for humans too."

—Touch the Earth

I

NOW IN THE DAWN

On a winter evening early in the month of January, 1974, I watched rain laden clouds move slowly across an almost full moon. Beyond the clouds, somewhere in the southwestern sky, the comet Kohoutek, dusty and dim, was threading its way through our destiny. The earth was suffering another war and the energy crisis, which was to become a lifestyle, was announced. I was aware of humanity moving swiftly through the cataclysm; some, perhaps, moving toward it and beginning to collide with the mistakes of the past.

Denourished food, a polluted environment, and the reckless waste of our natural resources now appear like lost reflections of mankind's blindness. Illness, want and inconvenience are stealing into once comfortable settings. Yet there are others who are mysteriously protected, who move through this strange death drama unharmed. I believe these are the people who have faith in the birth of a new age, and who have given their allegiance to the planet, to humankind, and to the dawning of consciousness.

Let me be clear from the beginning: this book is about revolution. It must be, for it is essentially about that which can heal us. I can no longer find the division between revolution and healing. The cry to change is being heard because the world is sick. If we do not heal the disease, we will die. In order to become well, we must change, and so revolution and healing flow together into a single act.

When I speak of revolution, I do not mean fighting in

the streets, blood spilt, or violence done. This is the way we have sought change in the past. Out of desperation, because people were not heard by those in power, the people have taken to arms and seized power. But now we are entering a new era. It is violence which we must leave behind. To maim and kill one another in order to bring change will only give us an illusion of change, while continuing in the same senseless patterns which have brought us to such misery. No, this is not a bloody revolution. This must be an inner change—a revolution of the mind.

This revolution of the mind and healing are intertwined because we cannot separate that which needs to be healed from that which is the cause of disease. Although our problems appear multiple, and disease seems to strike in a hundred different guises, there is only one basic cause at the source of all our ailments. The human race is suffering from a spiritual malaise. We have for too long neglected our souls. We have disobeyed the natural laws of the universe. We have ignored the intelligence and interrelationship of all beings and all species of life. Those whom we have entrusted with power have supported war, proliferated ignorance, and encouraged physical and spiritual laxity. Now we are reaping the bitter fruit of these dark seeds. Many people are sick, and the number of those who are ill continues to climb. Hearts are empty and souls are hungry for meaning. Some years back I heard a Hopi medicine man say that we must stay on the path of the Great Father, or suffer the consequences. We are presently witnessing those consequences. We are understanding at last that heaven and hell exist in the here and now, and that we have polluted paradise.

I begin this book in a dark mood, for all around me are indications of more misery to come. At the beginning of the energy crisis, the leaders of America made decisions which seem irreversible in their consequences. At a time when the whole ecological system was crying out for our loving attention, environmentalists and their concerns were pushed back, stalled and delayed. The excuse was that there were more immediate problems—a war, and an energy crisis. The real war is the one which mankind is waging on nature—through neglect, carelessness, ignorance and waste. And it is this war, this separation from the earth which is our home, which is bringing on the true crisis. It is inevitable that such divisive actions against nature will bring suffering.

Yet I am led on by a vision. Humanity has been promised an age of peace. In the midst of rubble and civilizations toppling, we are witnessing the dawning of an expanded consciousness. There is a light on the horizon. I have unshakable faith in this light. I know that we must move through the darkness, helping one another to the best of our ability, without ever losing sight of the clear vision which is calling us forward.

It is not unusual for me to hear people saying that it is impossible: we have made too many mistakes and the disaster is inevitable. Particularly in the cities one can hear these voices of despair—people who feel they are worthless, who think that their lives do not mean very much. These are the people who say, "Of course there are terrible things happening. I can see that. But what can *I* do?" There are so many who feel helpless against the mountain of corruption and ignorance. Each person feels alone against the tidal wave of darkness, their actions reduced to a futile and petty scrambling on a vast beach where there is no safety, and no possibility of escape.

We must first of all remember that we are not alone. The illusion that we are separate from one another is at the root of our troubled time. As soon as we begin to share our concerns, to voice our needs and express our dreams, we find ourselves linked to a thousand other beings with the same concerns, the same needs and the same dreams. There is no one person with the whole solution, or all the strength. The solution comes from each and all of us contributing what we know and what we love. In joining together we begin to puzzle out ways to act, to move, to change—and in this joining we find our strength, and our power.

We must also begin with ourselves, and in very simple ways. What can you do to make yourself healthier, stronger? In what ways can you make peace with yourself? Americans have come out of a tradition of striving and materiality. More often than not, happiness, for us, is always in the future. But happiness springs from within us, in this moment. It is not so much in external conditions, but in our *perception* of those conditions, that the answer lies.

I am not saying that external conditions do not matter, for this book is very much concerned with external conditions. Our environment always influences us and may, at times, be the determining factor in our lives. Yet true happiness remains a blend of internal and external factors. There is a marriage that takes place in the moment of joy—harmony is composed of union between thought and materiality.

If our external conditions are unpleasant, then hope lies in our belief in ourselves—in our capacity to change, affect and enhance our environment. If you are among those who feel trapped, who feels alone and unimportant, I urge you to try introducing into your own life the environmental changes, inner and outer, discussed in this book. If you feel strong and solid, secure in yourself, I urge you to find ways in which you can help make the healing environment a reality for all.

II

DÉJÀ VU AND FUTURE GLIMPSE

It is difficult to say when the sensation first began. As we drove into the city on a rainsoaked day in August my impressions were those of any traveler arriving in a large city. Struck by the traffic, the noise, the rapid tempo, this sudden movement and confusion was heightened after the long drive through quiet mountain landscapes which are the approach to Mexico City.

My first clear memory of the strange sensation was the following day, as I walked down a wide boulevard lined with trees. On both sides of the street were beautiful buildings. There were fountains, statues, a profusion of flowers wherever I looked. My first thought was that this avenue reminded me of the *Champs-Elysees* in Paris. But after several days in Mexico City I became aware that I was experiencing something I had felt in many European cities—it did not have to do with similarities in architecture, or landscape. Though I couldn't identify it, the feeling kept coming over me in waves.

It had been six years since I lived in Europe, and this was my first visit to a foreign country in all that time. Though I had many vivid memories of Europe, none of them explained this sense of *déjà vu*. It was not a sense of having been here before, but of having *felt* this before.

As the days passed I began to realize that the sensation was linked with the experience of beauty. Parks and gardens everywhere, exquisitely tiled floors and walls, quiet courtyards where lush plants grew, graceful stairwells, statues and fountains, buildings that were centuries old and pleasing because of their age—all this

16

made Mexico City beautiful in the way I had found many European cities beautiful. But knowing this did not help me solve the mystery of the deep stirring I felt walking through the city—a sense that I was different in this environment, as I had been different in Europe.

One afternoon we drove to a small town just south of Mexico City. We arrived near twilight, and stopped to walk around the plaza, in which there were three churches. I was drawn to the largest of these, a monumental cathedral built of huge red blocks of red-brown stone. I was stopped in the vestibule by an enormous bowl in the floor made of granite. The stone was heavy and entirely lacking in ornamentation. It was simply a container for clear water, but it felt like a forgotten offering to a giant deity. From both sides of the doorway leading into the interior of the church emerged two carved hands of heavy stone, cupped to hold holy water. These were also crude, as if they had been hewn out of rock by men who did not have a language. All this seemed so primitive that I somehow expected, once inside, to find myself standing on a dirt floor. But as I walked through the door my gaze was immediately drawn to the altar, and I realized that the few artifacts of the church had been deliberately and sensitively designed.

In concept and execution, the altar was so pure and light that it looked as if it had been lifted out of the twenty-fifth century and then had been placed, gently and without effort, in the midst of this cathedral silence. The altar was more a statement than a place—a statement made with a few simple, elegant strokes. The highly ornamental sacramental lamps I was used to seeing above the altar in Catholic churches, usually hung from heavy chains, were here represented by graceful half-ovals of polished brass, which held spheres of red glass in which candles flickered quietly. The cords which held these lamps were nearly invisible, so that at first glance the lamps seemed to be suspended in space. Above the unadorned altar there was a tall, narrow cross of dark wood. Again, there was no detail. It even lacked the traditional figure of Christ. The futuristic design of the altar seemed diametrically opposed to the ancient edifice which housed it, yet they complemented each other perfectly, for they were held together by a theme of stark simplicity and beauty. The building gave this effect by its crudity and immense stone weight, while the altar achieved the same effect with a lightness that was almost ephemeral, and a sophistication of design that seemed beyond our time.

The sensation that I had been experiencing in the city was, in this place, so strong that I felt overwhelmed by it. I had to know what I was feeling. I began to walk around the church, listening closely to what was inside, determined to stay in this cathedral until the mystery was solved. After walking in this way for awhile I realized that I felt bigger here. Though the size of the building should have emphasized my littleness, I felt instead that I was taller, somehow more expansive in both body and spirit. Then all at once one word struck me with such tremendous force that it felt like an inner explosion: dignity. It was a sense of dignity that I felt in this place, that I felt walking through the streets of Mexico City, that I remembered with longing when I thought of Europe.

For the first time, I saw clearly the incredible effect and impact of environment. In that moment, standing alone in the aisle of that church, I understood that people can be made to feel degenerate or divine by the mere fact of their physical environment. I saw everything around me as a reflection, and understood that we feel ourselves to be what our mirrors tell us we are. A sense of grace and beauty, of the nobility in mankind, our inspiration carved in stone or impressed in glass, our meditation on the fact of God left in wood or marble, love of line and form—all this echoed within, and gave me worth and meaning as I walked beneath the dome of the sky. I felt myself to be capable of these acts of creation, to be deserving of them. I was richer, for I had a heritage of divinity—stated and claimed by those who had created and built these beautiful cities.

And on the other end of this spectrum, I fully understood the depression I had experienced in many American cities. Memories crowded in on me now of too much chrome and plastic, vinyl and neon, paper cups and aluminum chairs, functional architecture that was empty of spirit or pride, pop ads blown up to giant billboard size, endless rows of houses all alike—a world where there was an infinity of cement, and less and less room for the green song of leaf and tree.

I retreat to the country repeatedly, and feel at home there. Still there is a great part of me that is urban, that loves machines and movement, the rhythm of civilization. But no matter how urban a person is, none of us is simply an efficient system. A person existing in an environment which is largely economical and functional is living in a desert. The spirit is starved.

That evening in Mexico I was still many years from reading G. I. Gurdjieff, who speaks of four foods that nourish us and that we must have—air, water, food and *image*. When I came across this concept in P. D. Ouspensky's book, *In Search of the Miraculous*, I knew what he meant, for I had felt it profoundly in my search that night to understand the meaning of my own emotions. Through image I had discovered dignity, and an affirmation of dignity in the human race. It is time, now, to take the key I found there and open the doors to a vision of environment which can heal humanity.

III

YOUR SELF AS A HEALING CENTER

My original impulse in writing this book was born in response to people who were deeply disturbed and trapped in dehumanized, nonsupportive institutions. I had amassed a great deal of material on the subject and was determined to find a way to present it meaningfully. But before I could even deal with the abstract nature of the material, I was interrupted by a visit from a friend.

Ann was depressed. She is in therapy, and defines herself as neurotic, sometimes even commenting on behavior in herself which borders on the psychotic. Her massive depression and sense of dissociation had been going on for several weeks. During that time I had seen very little of her, for I had found it difficult to relate to her. Instead I had spent some time mulling over her behavior and had made a note in my journal. "Ann is unwell because she is perpetually studying the nature of illness."

As we began talking, the distant being whose psyche I had commented upon became real again, became a person again. I remembered that Ann is a friend I care about, whose intelligence, warmth, and generosity I love. As she spoke I felt I was looking at a friend dying in front of my eyes. Her spirit was growing weaker each day, the fabric of her psyche becoming torn and tired. Depression was stealing over her like a dark, relentless fog. I wanted to shake her furiously, as a confrontation with death had once shook me. Look, I wanted to say, Look out the window at this day. The sun is shining, the air is clear and bright, the leaves are singing in the wind. There is love, there is joy, there are good meals with friends, there is warmth, there is the sound and smell of the ocean. Life is all around you and inside you, waiting to be lived. While you sink deeper and deeper into the hole of depression which is burying you, the day steals by, and then another, and another. One day you may wake up to find yourself old and bitter, asking yourself where your friends have gone, wondering where your hunger to taste the day has gone, groping futilely for love and the happiness that might have been.

I wanted not only to shake her, but also to wash the wounded spirit, nourish and feed the soul muscle, hone the will, and watch her come back to life again. I wanted to bathe her in light and stillness, to prescribe silence and meditation.

I left Ann, shaken by the emotions she had stirred, filled with enthusiasm about the concept of the healing center—a place where people in need, like Ann, could be nourished completely by everything, everyone, every act within the environment. It seemed natural to extend this simple caring for the individuals around me to a vision of how society might implement a new approach to the healing process—not a hospital, in which we are constantly reminded of illness, but a healing center, in which we are constantly reminded of health, our personal strength, dignity, and worth.

In our "normal" world we must all deal with the unpleasant effects of mechanization, pollution, and overpopulation. We all occasionally feel the need for something akin to the healing center. For that reason, I want to emphasize that each of you is capable of creating the healing environment in your own life, now. The healing centers of the future will be islands of sanity, beauty, and harmony. The healing centers of the present are those islands we create in our own sphere: the colors we wake to in the morning, the plants in our care who also care for us, the music that enriches our afternoon, the work that gives us substance and expression, the good food on our dinner table, and the laughter, honesty, peace and equality in our own relationships.

To heal our earth is an enormous task. But like the journey of a thousand miles that began with a single step, it is accomplished by each of you thinking on what you really want, and acting on it. In the constitution of the individual, the pursuit of wholeness is a right. Consider your own life, and the length of it. What have you given, what do you want to give? What do you receive? What do you want to receive? The healing process begins with each of you asking yourself these questions about the meaning of your life, and the way in which you want to live the space and time you have on earth. We do not need to accept oppression as a way of life, nor stand by helplessly watching it wear down and destroy others. The reach for autonomy begins by turning inward, contemplating our own heart and spirit. And in the same act we allow every other being the same autonomy, and work cooperatively to realize our dreams.

I hope that this book will inspire each of you to look at your own home, the spaces where you work, play, and study, and to find in yourself and your life those places which need nourishing. There is so much choice available to us if we simply begin with what is around us. It is a process of healing the negative energy that imprisons us, and strengthening the positive energy which frees us. And that process can begin in countless ways: learning to understand your dreams, changing the colors that you wear and that surround you, eating organic rather than chemical food, spending more time in the sunlight and less under fluorescent light, taking time regularly to exercise or dance, giving yourself space for silence and meditation. The self within knows what is needed for health, always. You need only to listen, for you are your own best doctor, and the creator of a personal environment which will extend harmony to those whose lives touch yours and to the rest of the community.

PART TWO

THE HEALING ENVIRONMENT

COUNTRY DOCTOR IN THE AQUARIAN AGE

(SHAMAN SONG)

On this green ridge of earth
I suffer the darkness
of my sojourn to the city.
Nothing can be
done
to heal my wound.
The medicine is in this place.

The birds rushing by
like a great wind
going south
will speak to my spirit,
the grass lush and wet
with winter rain
will speak to my spirit,

the gentle animal
who walks beside me
will speak to my spirit,
this rose-light path
where brown redwood needles
become earth
will heal my spirit,
this twilight air
breath of equilibrium
will heal my spirit.
Here,
between earth and sky,
here is my medicine.

Make me welcome now
my sisters, my brothers,
a shaman has come.
Give me earth and water
give me pure water,
clear air and firelight,
trees and rushing
water sound,
all this will make you well.

I will take the shape of stars
to light your mind
and pour color
from my battered leather bag
to renew you.
I will bottle this twilight
and release it
like balm
to soothe you.

I will ask for grace
and graceful motion
music
and the harmony of laughter,
the shape of spheres
and pyramids
for you to dwell in.

I will ask for gentle beings
who love all, all
who can sit quiet
and pray
they will be my staff
and they will befriend you.

In the fragrance of pine
and the ease of fern
in the exuberant lupine
and the gentle violet
in the sweet silent song
of the plants of this earth
in all this green wealth
I will nourish you.

Make me welcome now
my sisters, my brothers,
a shaman has come
and in all this
earth and sky,
fire and water,
is my medicine.

When we reach down to what is primitive in use, we understand greeting the rising sun as Father, and paying homage to the earth as Mother.

I

EARTH ENERGY

The Elements as Angels

tside the window of my bedroom I can see the
aluma River. A crude bridge spans its glittering sur-
e, water birds glide above it, a small boat with red and
ite sails takes advantage of the strong wind. Last night
full moon came up over the river, a deep orange
be serenely rising to preside over the night sky. I
'e seen the surface of the water change in countless
ys, as the light of the day changes, as the weather
nges. Yet in turning to look at this body of water I am
'ays assured of its ability to heal and calm, to put me
touch with deeper voices in myself. Water has great
wer. In reflecting on that power a flood of memories is
ked, and I remember all the elements, the seasons of
life, and the ways in which nature has healed me,
in and again.

arth stirs a distant memory of myself as a child, sit-
g happily in the newly turned dirt of my mother's
den with the morning sun on my skin. There I was
tent with the simple act of loosening the soil with my
ds, feeling its warmth and rough texture in my palm,
watching it slip through my fingers to return again to
th.

ast winter it was firelight that brought this sense of
er quiet and the tranquility of contemplation. I spent
ny long evenings sitting and watching the fire in the
od stove, listening for hours to the play of my
ughts as the firelight danced and rain spilled on the
f.

Air, which we live with daily and often take for granted, at times touches me in a way which makes me distinctly aware of the intimacy of our relationship. One spring morning on a mountaintop in Tasahara, while playing t'ai chi, I had a sense of the wind being my partner, dancing around me and through me, the two of us exhilarating in this sharing and contact.

Earth, Air, Fire and Water, in ancient texts, are four angels which can minister health to mankind. They are another aspect of the healing environment which can and should be used consciously as healing agents. As I remember the ways in which the elements have healed me, I find myself thinking of people as tribal. We are the human tribe. Beneath our civilized masks we are linked by blood and bone, by our animal nature. By animal I do not mean our "lower" nature. Earth is holy, as well as Heaven. When we reach down to what is primitive in us, we understand greeting the rising sun as Father, and paying homage to the earth as Mother. Primitive people live in relationship with the elements, with nature. They understand the need for respect and reverence in that relationship. Civilized man has stressed control of the elements to such a degree that he has nearly obliterated this relationship, and is consequently dangerously close to obliterating himself. We are beginning to understand that we are in no way apart from, or superior to, nature. Everything is linked, every part is interdependent, every organism and thing has a function and is meaningful to the whole. We cannot mistreat any part of nature without suffering the consequences. If we are to heal the violence we have already done to our environment, and if we are to understand the ways in which our environment can heal us, we must return to a loving relationship with nature.

The healing process is aided by exposure to an environment in which meaning is present. The simplest way to achieve this is to include nature, for a sense of meaning permeates nature. There is order and intelligence in the seasons changing, sunrise and sunset, the flowering of the bud. In all these aspects of nature lies the potential for awakening a realization of the Self, for reminding us of our true nature and thus enabling us to grasp the sense of joy which is beyond the clash of opposites. There is something curiously tangible about happiness. It is as if happiness brings us to experience our senses on the deepest possible level. The fragrance of the first narcissus is not only delightful in itself; it fills us with the remembrance of spring—the whole miracle is recurring, and we, in this intake of sweet air, are part of it.

I remember being with a friend in Los Angeles one April. We were on vacation, and had intended to stay in the city nearly a week, but after two days we had to leave—we both felt unable to breathe in the heavy air, unable to see because of the smog. We drove to the Big Sur country north of the city and there I felt overwhelmed by the purity of the air and the intensity of spring—lush new green grass, clear water running in the streams, the opulent beauty of hillsides carpeted with purple and white lupine. "The people in the city have forgotten this," my friend remarked. Her statement was simple, and true people have forgotten the power of life itself to move the heart, awaken the mind, to impregnate us with a sense of joy. As people forget they become numb, they become like sleepwalkers. It is easy to command people in their sleep, to tell them what they want and to substitute a facsimile of life for the real thing.

This experience in the Big Sur country brought to mind a similar one that had occurred in San Francisco. The smog had been very heavy for several days. One night it rained—a downpour that lasted for hours. The next morning dawned on a sparkling San Francisco with clear blue skies and billowing white clouds. The streets were newly washed, and an autumn wind blew in from the ocean. The cold clean air revealed brightly painted houses, gardens and flowers blooming, multi-colored rooftops. Here was the real city. The other seemed a bad dream which people walked in daily, unable to awake. I wondered how many people experienced this sense of translucent meaning, this delight in the fact of a clear, glorious morning. And how long was it before we forgot our delight in the routine of the day—the business of the "real" world?

One way to define a breakdown is in the incapacity to deal with that "real" world. During such times the psyche is demanding that we touch center—home base. To do that most successfully people need to be in spaces which allow them time to give attention to the inner processes. The presence of nature, the nearness of it in those spaces is intrinsically important to healing the inner processes.

How can we use the elements in our own healing process? The first answer that comes to mind is that they must be integrated into our activity. In finding a prescription for health and well-being, all the different aspects of the environment must be used, in whatever mixture seems alchemically right for the individual. Each of the elements represents a different function in the human being, and each suggests certain activity.

The Elements and the Anatomy of Consciousness

According to ancient tradition, the four elements represented four different aspects of man. Air was symbolic of the thinking faculty, and in present anatomy is the "new brain" located in the cerebral cortex. In psychocybernetic language it is the conscious mind which programs the subconscious computer. Water was symbolic of the emotions, which in present anatomy is controlled by the hypothalamus, or the "old brain." This is also called the subconscious mind. Earth was symbolic of matter—the physical body itself. Fire represented spirit. It is the vital principle, the soul of the individual. In Chinese philosophy there are five elements, and in addition to the four aspects discussed here, we must also include a fifth—Jung's transcendent function, the Self which is ultimate consciousness, capable of balancing and integrating the other four aspects.

The Elements and Activity

Earth: We need earth to work in, and to work with. The idea of work here is not one of monetary energy in exchange for time and services. It is a more basic exchange of energy, and a relationship in which nourishment is tangible.

Since earth is substance, its use is especially beneficial for those who are abstracted or too identified with mental processes. It may be useful also for people who feel their life is superficial, and who have been for a long time in situations where life appears false or shallow. Such a person needs to dig into the earth, to watch a seed become a living plant, and to know that he is needed to water that green life, to tend it, and care for it. In such a tangible relationship is much symbolic material, for it is an external expression of the inner nurturing that needs to go on within the individual. The simple fact of being out in the open air and sunlight while working in the earth is healing and strengthening for both body and spirit.

The concept of working with the earth can be extended to creative expression for those who wish to sculpt, to work with clay and pottery. Creative expression might more properly be called water activity, since it is essentially an emotional release. But by providing actual media—matter—as an outlet for emotions, we combine and integrate the two elements. There are many kinds of media available for creative release. John Perry's work in this area has shown that such creative expression, as a means to communicate the inner life, can be deeply valuable in helping a person to reintegrate and renew herself.

Air: Air is so basic to our being alive that we are hardly cognizant of it. But the fact is that we are alive only so long as we are breathing. When inhalation and exhalation stop, the body dies. It is unnecessary to quote here the vast amount of material that shows what we breathe and how we breathe deeply affects our being.

As air is representative of the thinking function, its use would be recommended for those who feel their thinking is scattered, disorganized, or in other ways unclear, and also for those who dwell too much in sensation or are drowned in emotions.

Both yoga and t'ai chi ch'uan are excellent physical disciplines which use air to change and strengthen all the vital functions. These physical systems of integration both include the idea of vital energy in the air we breathe. Yogis call this prana, the t'ai chi student knows it as chi. It is invisible, and yet it is the substance, the stuff, the vital principle of all life. The channeling of this vital energy, replenishing and increasing its store in our bodies, is only one of the benefits we can draw from t'ai chi and yoga. Both systems strengthen the body and increase longevity, calm and clarify the mind, develop the will, and tend to foster positive emotions.

In thinking about air and its relationship to health, it is important to know about and consider the effects of negative and positive ions. What are ions? They are molecules. Positive ions have missing electrons, negative ions have extra electrons. Clean air is loaded with ions. In places where the air is clear and gets you "high," there are more negative ions. Think for a moment of the places where people go to rest, to heal themselves, or to live in a healthy environment—mountains, the countryside, beaches, islands, forests, and places where there are lakes, rivers, and creeks. Health spas, European sanitoriums, national parks and gardens, resorts—these are the pleasant places of the earth. And in all of them you find a high concentration of negative ions.

In today's world there is an increasing amount of space in which positive ions are concentrated, and in these places we find the clear-wind, clear-mind state becoming its opposite: depression, irritability, fatigue, poor health, and negative emotions in general (even to the point of violence) are the result of concentrated positive ions. Dr. David Galin, in an interview I read some time ago, when asked where the "bad" places are, answered:

> Cities. The middle of smog in cities. Or big office buildings where air is constantly recirculated and feels so dead. There are a lot of evil winds that are well-known around the world: the Mistral, and there is one that blows out of the desert across Israel. In the time of these winds the people get crazy, there is much more illness, suicide rates go up. Judges give lenient sentences because they know that this is a difficult time. It turns out the winds are full of positive ions. And a lot of the centers of mystical teaching in the past have been placed at sites where there were natural sources of negative ions.[1]

Natural and holistic healing can happen wherever there is an awareness and application of the basic principles discussed in this book. I want to encourage those people who live in urban areas and wish to create the healing environment for themselves—in their homes, neighborhoods, and the places where they work or learn. I urge these people to use this book as a guide, to look at the gestalt of their own environments and find those aspects which need attention. Every individual and each group of people will find their own framework, structure, and basic expression.

For those people who live in cities, however, air is a very important factor, and the presence of negative ionizers may be helpful. Negative ionizers are small, relatively simple machines which increase negative ions in the air. They are already widely used in Canada, Europe, England, Russia, and Israel. They are used in hospitals, stores, private homes, automobiles, and offices. It has been reported that their use concentrates healing time for burns, so that even severe burns heal faster with less pain and less scarring. They have been shown to bring people out of depressed and anxious states, and to reduce the occurrence of respiratory illness.

Negative ionizers are not widely known in America. At present, it is illegal for them to be sold in interstate commerce, and the Food and Drug Administration has prohibited any claims that the ionizers have any health benefits whatsoever. The FDA refuses to accept the results of research done in other countries (described in one pamphlet as "voluminous") Nor, to my knowledge, is there any wide-scale research being done in this country.

I suspect that this state of affairs cannot go on for long, and that once people find out about ionizers they will create a demand for them, and certainly insist that we research their effects. There is every indication that they can benefit people who live in cities, and especially help those who work with illness in any form.

Water: "With the exception of pure air, there is no other element of nature that is as important in sustaining life as pure water."[2] Since water is representative of our emotional nature, its use is beneficial for those whose emotions are sluggish, violent, repressed, or undeveloped. Water clarifies, purifies, and renews us. Its use as a healing agent suggests many possibilities. In thinking of diet, the availability of *pure* water is very important. Baths should also be included in the healing process, particularly in dealing with tension. As a medium which relaxes, cleanses, and renews energy, the bath is a simple and powerful cure. Becoming familiar with the work of herbalists who know the effects of different herbs added to bath water can deepen the benefits of your bath. Whenever possible take advantage of pools where you can swim, play, and exercise. Remember that steam baths and saunas purify the body by eliminating poisons through the pores—we must think of cleansing and washing the interior as well as the exterior body.

During an herbalist retreat this spring I met Suevo Brookin, an herbalist who is very much involved with hydrotherapy (cold water therapy) He gave a convincing lecture on the benefits of hydrotherapy and a clear, simple explanation of its appropriate use. I have since tried using cold water in the ways Suevo recommended and am personally impressed with the positive results. Cold water is definitely a part of healthful living, and it is too easily forgotten in our super-comfortable society.

Suevo urged that whenever hot water had to be used (hot baths, for instance), herbs should always be added to the water. As a transition to a real hydrotherapy program, Suevo recommended that people note how much hot and cold water they use in their lives, and begin gradually introducing more and more cold water in place of hot water. He also objected to the heating and chlorination of public swimming pools, and said that both heat and chlorine negate the beneficial results of swimming. When I asked how pools which would be used by many people might be kept sanitary in a natural way (without the addition of chemicals) one person in the audience said that a friend used a black light in his pool to cleanse it. This may well be the answer. (See Chapter on Light and Life for the benefits of black or ultraviolet light.)

We need to take advantage of meditative pools and ponds, quiet bodies of water to look into and contemplate wherever and whenever they are available. Meditative pools suggest depth and calm, they can quiet the turmoil within by the silent eloquence of their being. The presence of modest aquariums is also helpful, for watching water beings can inspire and soothe us. Since running water increases the negative ions in the air, fountains have the natural beneficent effects of a brook or stream. And to watch the play and dance of water in a fountain, to listen to it rush over stone, can be truly curative; it can inspire us and lighten the emotional timbre of the whole organism.

Fire:

> Fire is one of the most ancient and effective symbols . . . On the purely human level it is a symbol of heat, of protection from cold, and defense from wild animals for primitive man. Also it is a symbol of transformation processes—of cooking, of the changing and purification of raw materials and minerals; therefore it is an important chemical symbol connected with transmutation and sublimation. Further, it is a symbol of destruction, of danger; and finally it is one of the purest—if not the purest of all—symbols of the spirit, both the spirit in man ascending toward the universal spirit, and of "fire coming down from heaven."[3]

Fire is a powerful symbol, one which is especially helpful for those whose spirits are neglected or abused, who are too identified with the thinking faculty or caught up in sensation.

The presence of a fireplace can be a great aid to the healing process. Simply to watch firelight, to be near its warmth, can rest the mind and heal the emotions. There is something so primitive, so primordial, in our relation to fire that it is difficult to communicate what it is that happens while watching logs burn, or embers sparking. And very deep, ancient images and emotions are stirred in the tending of a fire—in gathering wood and building a fire. We understand something of our origins in this activity.

The most powerful image of fire is the sun itself—solar fire. The sun is the center, the heart of our solar system. It is the source of spiritual nourishment; it quickens, warms, and engenders life. It is consciousness, it is the father principle. Sunbaths, walking and exercising in the sunlight, are not only pleasant activities. They are a necessary part of one's environment in maintaining good health, and an important activity in recovering health. It is good to remember the wisdom of the old Italian proverb: "Dove il sol non entra, entra il dottore." (Where the sun does not enter, the doctor does.)[4]

Summary

Many uses of the elements which I have been suggesting here are extremely simple. They seem obvious.

Any person who is concerned with well-being and maintaining physical and emotional health uses the elements; yet we exclude them in thinking of healing the unbalanced mind or the diseased body. Medicine is limited to something that comes in bottles or in pill form. We need to remove these restrictions and narrow boundaries, these strictly limited definitions of medicine. Expansion is the keyword. Once we have opened our minds to include the elements as healing agents, as angels which can minister help, then there are countless ways in which they can be used. This brief chapter is only a minute beginning. We have just cracked open the door to glimpse a universe.

Since the dawn of humanity, plants, trees and flowers have always, without ever being asked, been there to cure, feed, lighten, cheer, refresh, renew, protect us. We must learn to know these beings better, and consciously include them as fellow healers in our work.

The Subtle Healers

Humanistic psychology has created many new and exciting approaches to healing. It has also rediscovered and is fostering many ancient ways of healing. In addition to the many fine psychotherapeutic methods we now have available, we need to consider the plant life of this earth, its ability to help us, and to support the healing process. In plants we find our original medicines. A complete exploration of the healing effects of plant life could easily compose a book, and there is an abundance of material on this subject. Here, I wish only to stir memories, offer suggestions, and perhaps awaken the reader to the wonderful possibilities.

Everyone has, I am certain, had at least one experience of nature that was affirmative—at least one experience that brought a moment of beauty, of at-one-ment, a sense of awe and of the mystery of being. It is not necessarily the scope of that experience that makes it a whole-making one. We can be affirmed by the open sea, expanded by the stark, awesome contours of a mountain wilderness. Yet even the flowering of a small garden can bring joy and a sense of completeness. Nature can plunge us into a plane deeper than the reaches of the intellect, into a state beyond analysis, where we know in the very center of our being what life *is*. In that *isness* is meaning.

Today it is raining here. Perhaps these are the last heavy rains of winter, pelting down out of a sky thick with grey clouds. In this quarter of the earth spring is already trembling on the edge, on the brink of that wild plummet into full, riotous flower. I gaze lovingly at the orchards with their rows of tiny fruit trees—black, barren, and glistening in the rain. Beneath the trees with their jagged winter branches a rich green carpet of spring grass is already present, and overnight thousands

of tiny bright flowers have appeared, a feast of yellow
extending for miles. These are the images that bring a
sense of inner renewal, just as the spring season renews
the earth.

Spring has always symbolized the upsurge of new life.
It awakens hope, the expectancy of better things, the
energy that enables us to go on, no matter what darkness
the winter may have brought. And so each season has its
message, its own way of centering us, of putting us in
touch with ourselves and the meaning of natural cycles
in our lives. Just as the seasons all have their particular
function and meaning within us, so the different vari-
eties of plant life have their unique message, their simple yet profound ways of healing. It is only necessary for
us to be in tune, to be quiet enough, receptive enough to
hear—to take the time to reach out and touch, or perhaps
to let ourselves be touched by, the green energy of this
planet.

Some time ago I heard of a woman who began distort-
ing reality to such an extent that people who knew her
became disturbed. When the symptoms persisted, and
no one was able to help, her family was contacted and
arrangements were made to have her committed to an
institution. Upon learning that this had been done, one
friend quietly remarked, "I don't think she needs to go to
an institution. I think she needs some time to sit on a
hillside for awhile and think things over."

To the sophisticated mind it seems too simple a remedy. But guided by feeling, listening to that voice inside
which we know to be our heart speaking, this remedy
makes infinite sense. Perhaps it is only because we have
become so urbanized and civilized that we have forgotten the natural and instinctive healing processes. Have
you never gained new perspective on your life by looking at the expanse of earth from a hilltop, or been
quieted by the murmur of the sea at night? Have you
never been made to feel better by the sound of a brook

singing in your ears all afternoon, or been answered by
the sun breaking out of a clouded sky? In the simplest
attributes of nature there is power. Even dew shining on
a spiderweb can remind us that there is meaning and
purpose in life.

I am not saying that curing an illness, whether it be of
body or mind, is as simple as letting a person dwell in a
beautiful green setting—only that it would help the
healing process. We can draw sustenance from the earth,
strength from a tree, solicitude from a plant. In creating
the healing environment we must remember to include
this subtle yet powerful voice of nature.

"There is a wonderful science in nature, in trees,
herbs, roots and flowers, which man has never yet
fathomed."[5] These are the words of Jethro Kloss, who
wrote a book called *Back to Eden*. His book is a treasure
house of natural healing remedies, and it is my personal
home and herbal handbook for any kind of illness. Although he never bore the initials M. D. after his name,
Jethro Kloss was a true doctor, one who knew how to
help the body heal itself, and how to live a life that
prevented illness. Among other things, his book gives
careful instructions in how to prepare fomentations and
compresses, explains the basic principles and uses of
massage, talks about the curative power of water and the
various baths to be used in treating the sick, and gives an
incredibly complete guide to herbs and their specific
use in treating various diseases. A simple reading of
Jethro Kloss's index alone is enough to make you realize
that there is a natural remedy for any and every illness.

Western medicine has become synonymous with
drugs, and because of this most people are unfamiliar
with natural remedies and the medicinal properties of
plants. We have come to rely on the medicine that comes
in pill form, or that is shot into us via an injection. Drugs
act so quickly that it is easy to see why they are thought
of as "miracle cures," but it is becoming increasingly

evident how dangerous they can be, as many people now die of an adverse reaction to drugs or develop more complicated illnesses as a result of drugs used to treat an original illness. In addition to the possible harm they can do, drugs teach us nothing about the cause of our illness, and they often give us a false illusion of health. The symptoms of the common cold, for instance, are uncomfortable because they are your body's way of telling you about accumulated toxins, and they are an attempt by your body to expel those toxins. Instead of helping the body by resting and fasting, drinking fresh fruit juices and herbal teas that help to eliminate these toxins (Kloss lists no less than thirty-eight herbs that are useful in treating colds), most people keep right on working, continue to eat the devitalized foods that no doubt helped bring on the cold, and swallow cold pills that repress the uncomfortable symptoms.

People have come to rely too much on doctors and drugs. We are led to believe that illness is some outside enemy force that comes unbidden (and that we can conquer with a drug). The truth is that our own lifestyle—the way we live, think, eat, and drink—is the determining factor in health or illness. There must be a receptive *environment* for illness to occur, and we are responsible for creating that environment in ourselves.

It is not only the use of herbs rather than pills that I am speaking of in this chapter. I mean that the presence of certain plant life—just its presence—can help to effect cures. There is current speculation that in the future there will be "healing gardens." It has been discovered, for instance, that being near deep red roses helps poor blood circulation. Doctors have for years recommended living in pine forests for those with heart conditions. Joseph Weed, who has written extensively on psychic energy and means of employing it, maintains that pine trees store psychic energy, and that we can renew and increase our own store by simple contact with the pine.

Ferns are cooling and restful. People who are excitable or suffering from nervous distress would benefit from the presence of ferns. In tropic climates there is a powerful life force surging through in the brilliance and abundance of exotic plant life. Rooms where many tropic plants are present are particularly useful in restoring vitality. Certain flowers that bloom in spring are somehow cheering, inherently joyful, and these may, in part, be an answer to alleviating depressed states. All plant life must, in this way, be explored for its potential use in healing illness.

We need to remember that we are in a vital and intimate relationship with plant life—that we are anatomically dependent on plant life. It is the plant life of this earth that makes oxygen available to us. The depletion of plant life in cities is a major factor in the cause of frequent and deep states of depression in city dwellers. Both body and psyche are suffering from too much carbon dioxide.

Since the dawn of humanity, plants, trees, and flowers have always, without ever being asked, been there to cure, feed, lighten, cheer, refresh, renew, protect us. We must learn to know these beings better, and consciously include them as fellow healers in our work.

We should make every effort to establish an intelligent relationship with light, for light and life are synonymous.

II

COLOR THERAPY AND THE HUMAN AURA

It is of the utmost importance that we should cultivate the right colour vibrations in and around our bodies and surroundings. A great deal of the discord and incompatibility between members of families and groups of people closely associated together is caused by cross-vibrations which are aroused by the predominance of some one or more inharmonious colours within some personal aura or environment.

—S. G. J. Ouseley
The Power of the Rays

In the book *Winged Pharoah* by Joan Grant, the high priest of the Pharoah, Ptah-kefer, explains to the royal children the way in which he sees aura:

With our earth eyes we cannot see patience, or anger, or jealousy, or greed; we can only see the reactions of them. But if I look at a man with the eyes of the spirit, I can see his thoughts, perhaps I should say his emotions, as colour; and the darker the colour, the nearer he is to Earth; and the paler the colour, the nearer he is to the source of light, to which one day we must all attain.

Jealousy and greed I see as a dull dark green; but true sympathy, which is compassion, is the pale green of the sky before dawn. Wisdom is a pale clear yellow, like sunshine on a white wall; deceit, and lust for riches, are clay-coloured, like the mud from which bricks are baked. And in the same way every kind of emotion has its special shade, and those that are most often experienced determine the colour of the light that shines from each of us. But fear clouds the colours with a dirty grey, like oily smoke; and fierce impatience flecks them with a red, like little drops of blood. There are many other signs like these, by which I can judge a man. . . .[6]

For centuries psychics have reported that we have two bodies—a spiritual, or soul body, as well as a physical body. For one who is trained in extrasensory perception, this spiritual body, commonly known as the human aura, has visible form and can be seen as a field of color around the physical body. *Psychic Discoveries* points out that clairvoyants feel that the aura is actually a misnomer.

. . . they believe the human body is interpenetrated by another body of energy and it is the luminescence from this *second* body radiating outward that they see as aura. We look, they say, something like an eclipse of the sun by the moon, the luminous astral body being completely concealed by the physical body.[7]

Kirlian photography, developed by Samyon Davidovitch Kirlian, has given scientists the equivalent of a "spiritual eye" with which they can see this second body. Kirlian photography has clearly demonstrated that everything, animate and inanimate, has a second energy field, that in living organisms this astral body clearly reflects the well-being or illness of the physical body, and that it takes on the dominant characteristics of a person's inner life.

> In living things, we see the signals of the inner state of the organism reflected in the brightness, dimness and color of the flares. The inner life activities of the human being are written in these "light" hieroglyphs. We've created an apparatus to write these hieroglyphs. But to read them we're going to need help.[8]

Clearly one of the most immediate sources of help is from the occult scientists who were recording the interpretations of psychics long before Kirlian photography was discovered. One of the most startling books in this area is *Thought Forms* by Annie Besant and C. W. Leadbeater.

Thought Forms is a rather complex study of the different "bodies" of man and of the different planes of matter. It explains that thoughts are composed of vibrations and that these vibrations gather etheric matter (the "stuff" of the astral plane) to produce an actual form, and that these forms are the images clairvoyants see around human beings. The nature of the thought produces the kind of form, and the kind and intensity of the emotion accompanying the thought determines the color, or colors, of the form. The book is well illustrated, and depicts thought forms seen around different individuals by psychics. These illustrations tend to give you a different sense of yourself and of the "visibility" of your inner life.

The authors of *Thought Forms* speak of the correspondence between scientific studies and theosophical studies in researching color. Kirlian photography also underscores the findings of occult experimentation. Both the scientific and the occult literature convinced me that color is an important element in healing.

We all know color plays a significant part in our lives. It affects our decisions and feelings to an amazing degree. But to date, industry and advertising have probably made greater use of color knowledge than has medicine. In designing an environment beneficial to well-being, important consideration should be given to colors. If emotions can produce color, then certainly the reverse is true—color can produce an emotion, or affect or change emotional states.

At the time I was first researching color I had little to go on. In *Winged Pharoah,* Ptah-kefer, the high priest, speaks of the "highest expression" of three colors:

> . . . the pale clear yellow of Wisdom, which is all experience; the gentle green of Compassion, which is perfect understanding; the true scarlet of the Warriors of Maat, which is Courage that is beyond fear.[9]

From this description it appears red is important in treating illness which has fear as a source, that yellow can clarify and calm mental illness, that green will bring a sense of compassion and sympathy to someone suffering grief. The book *Thought Forms* had also impressed me strongly with the sense of ambience which characterizes colors as seen on the astral plane (this is particularly true of colors emanating from positive, harmonious emotions and high spirituality). Light showing through a color is a way of increasing its effectiveness. (We all know the sense of wonder and well-being that can be awakened by sunlight suddenly pouring through stained glass.)

Color and Music in the New Age, by Corinne Heline, gives a complete description of the use of color in healing which is based on the zodiac. The different planets are traditionally associated with different colors (and with different numbers) and certain signs govern various parts of the body. Since this astrological approach to color healing correlated with approaches in other literature (occult, parapsychological, and books by other color therapists), I compiled a Color Healing Chart based on this zodiacal concept. (The chart can be found on the back cover of this book, and instructions for its use are at the end of this chapter.)

For those who are interested in a very complete and detailed application of color in treating body, mind, emotions and spirit, Corinne Heline's chapter called "Color Significance of the Twelve Zodiacal Signs" is especially recommended. She gives a good brief summary of the therapeutic value of colors in the following:

> From the standpoint of their therapeutic value, the reds are stimulating and invigorating to man's physical body. The yellows vitalize and accelerate his mental activities. The greens are restful and soothing to his nervous system. The blues are inspirational, giving spiritual tone to his whole composition. The purples accelerate and sublimate all the processes of his body, mind and spirit.[10]

A study of color healing quickly reveals that there is a color available to treat all conditions—whether physical, mental, or emotional—and which we now, for the most part, treat only with drugs. In Europe, particularly in England, much greater use has been made of color in healing. The fact that we have made so little use of it in America is another indication of western medicine's narrow approach to health—we rely heavily on drugs, bottled medicine, pills and surgery, rather than taking advantage of what is readily and naturally available in the environment.

Color is everywhere. Try to imagine the world without color. It is difficult, if not impossible. Wherever you are at this moment, look around. How many colors, shades and hues of primary colors can you see?

Now think of yourself—not your physical body, but the invisible you—your aura, which is a luminous body of color. When your physical body is sick, or imbalanced,

the aura indicates the imbalance by color, more specifically, it indicates the kind of illness by muddied color, or
lack of color. When we use color in healing, we take a
direct route to the aura, which in turn translates the
(newly) balanced condition to the physical body.

If you will take a little time to learn the basic relationship between the colors of the spectrum and the parts of
the body which those colors treat, you can do a great deal
for yourself in dealing with simple ailments. For instance, if you find yourself under great pressure and in
an agitated state because of it, you would apply your
knowledge by wearing cool colors, particularly blue, or a
soft green. I recommended to a friend of mine who was
undergoing a period of depression that he not wear any
dark colors for the time being. I suggested he wear light
colors, especially blue and violet (or lavender), as these
would help to balance out his "dark" feelings. The cause
and cure of his depression was far more complicated
than just changing the color of his shirts, but he later
reported that this assisted him in his recovery. In China,
the color traditionally worn for mourning is white. This
is very wise, because white is associated with clarity,
spiritual enlightenment, and peace. The western habit of
wearing black for mourning only increases the grief felt
at someone's dying, and the longer it is worn the more
difficult it is to move away from morbid thoughts and a
sense of loss.

Another book which is very helpful in understanding
the role of color in healing is S. G. J. Ouseley's *The
Power of the Rays: The Science of Colour Healing.* Although Ouseley does not base his color theory on the
zodiac, he and Corinne Heline are basically in agreement about color therapy. Ouseley presents a theory of
color healing and practice, goes into detail about the
human aura, the physical body, and the etheric body,
and gives simple explanations on the use of color in healing. He talks about the application of color through color
lamps (and how to obtain or construct these lamps), the

use of color massage, and how one can "charge" food, clothing, and water (for drinking or bathing) with the appropriate color. He outlines, in a very practical way, several simple color healing methods, and includes meditations on the different colors. Ouseley's book is an excellent one for the individual who wants to understand and use color in his own life. Conscious use of the therapeutic properties of color will enrich the aesthetic experience of color. The color, or colors, present in the rooms where a person stays or spends great quantities of time should be carefully considered.

Corinne Heline mentions several times the use of color in England to treat patients during the war, especially soldiers suffering from shock and/or fear. *Psychic Discoveries* states that research in diagnosing illness through the aura is still continuing in Europe. In Switzerland, at the Lukas Clinic in Dornach, color is being used in the treatment of cancer. The fact that color is important both in diagnosing illness and treating it does not have to be proven. Knowledge of the healing properties of color needs only to be disseminated and used. We need to explore the possibilities of color healing in depth, for the different hues evolving from the basic spectrum all have their particular beneficial qualities. As mentioned, on the back cover of this book is a Color Healing Chart. The planets for each astrological sign, and the signs of the zodiac, are indicated at the outer edge of the circle. Each section of the circle indicates the color associated with that astrological sign. Within the color sections I have listed either parts of the body/ psyche, or different illnesses, which that color heals. Your astrological sign is *not* important in using this chart. The condition, or part of the body, which you want to heal is the important factor. (No matter what sign you are, if you have a heart condition, it will respond favorably to the orange-gold of Leo; if you have insomnia, the green of Cancer or the yellow of Libra will help you to sleep; if your appetite is poor, touches of the Aries red at the table will help to activate the appetite.) There are also key words listed in the chart, such as "illumines," "love," "transmutes." With these words I have attempted to convey the essence of the activity of each color. These key words are not meant to limit the activity of the color, but only to give a certain feeling for the color. This chart is very limited due to space, therefore the information given within each color section is far short of what might be there. It is meant to serve only as a beginning for those who are interested in color and healing.

I have so often heard people say that "green is a healing color" or "blue is a healing color." *All* colors have healing properties. To use color wisely, one must understand these properties and the context in which the color is to be used. Moderation is always a good guide, and you must use your own good judgment and common sense in the degree and extent to which you use any color for its therapeutic value. There are always several approaches to introducing a color into your life—use what feels comfortable for you. (For instance, if you want to use the Libra yellow to cure insomnia, you might wear yellow to bed, use yellow sheets or a yellow bedspread, or even paint your bedroom yellow. If you are involved in a group endeavor, meditate with your group on the radiant Aquarian blue. If your group does not meditate together, then when you are working with them, surround them mentally in a cloud of this Aquarian blue.)

This chart is designed to act only as a simple guide. If you really want to use color as a healing agent, please investigate the literature which is available. The English authors and specialists from India are most helpful. The books which I could obtain by Faber Birren, a noted American psychologist who works with color, I found fairly uninspiring. This may have been due to the particular works I read, or because of Dr. Birren's approach, which is basically behavioral. In any case, I urge you to read the available literature thoroughly. If you can, find people who really know color and its use in healing. They are always happy to share their knowledge.

Unless you are working under the guidance of a true color therapist, do not lay the burden of your ills on color and expect it to fix everything. Just changing a color in your surroundings is not enough to change your life or heal a serious illness. It can most certainly help and you should use color intelligently and to your advantage when a condition needs to be put in balance or brought back to harmony.

If you want to work on yourself when you are ill, depressed or feel out of balance, approach the problem *environmentally*. Look at the total picture—think on each aspect of yourself, your lifestyle, your internal and external environment. What is lacking, what needs changing, what needs nourishment? Is it the food you eat, the way you think (your attitudes and beliefs) lack of rest, lack of activity, avoidance of certain issues, people or conditions which are causing stress, the kind and quality of light around you, the colors in your life? It is always a combination of elements that brings on imbalance, and you should use a combination of healing approaches in working on yourself. Integrate the approaches which feel right to you to regain a harmonious life environment.

Rainbow Meditation

For those who want to incorporate the benefits of color through meditation, I would like to share this simple "Rainbow Meditation." The images arose spontaneously after experiencing The Rainbow Show at the De Young Museum in San Francisco.

1. Quiet yourself by sitting or lying down and allowing the body to relax. Let the breath become deep, even, and slow. Still the senses.

2. Allow your spirit-self to leave the body.

3. See yourself drifting upward, across the sky, until you are floating easily above a calm, sparkling blue ocean.

4. Before you is a rainbow. Drift through the seven colors of the spectrum, taking time to gently bathe in each of the colors. As each color permeates your body, be conscious of the particular benefits this color brings to you, spiritually and physically.

5. When you emerge from the rainbow, become aware of the sun, and the warm, bright, golden-white light it transmits. Feel yourself in the center of one of the sun's rays, and dry/wash yourself in this brilliant sunlight.

6. See your spirit-self returning and merging once more with your physical body.

Key: Red ...... *body/vitality/life force*
Orange ... *life and energy to the body/ strengthens/renews*
Yellow ... *thought/clear mentality/the five senses*
Green .... *harmony/health/abundance/ renewal/rest*
Blue ..... *spiritual peace*
Indigo ... *intuition*
Violet .... *body-spirit/earthly understanding/ wisdom*

III

STRUCTURAL DESIGN AND GEOMETRIC SYMBOL

Dwelling Space and Consciousness

To date, the healing effects of structural design is an area which has had very little formal experimentation. My own interest in it was sparked by *Psychic Discoveries Behind the Iron Curtain,* in which a book called *Ondes des Formes (Waves from Forms)* by L. Turenne is mentioned. Turenne asserts that various forms, ". . . such as spheres, pyramids, semi-spheres, squares—act as different types of *resonators* for the energy of the cosmos, the sun, and the energy all around us."[11] The same article goes on to say that certain of these forms would have a healthful effect on humans, specifically citing the sphere, the pyramid, and the geodesic dome.

Two Experiments

This statement about healthful geometric forms first triggered my concept of using structural design in healing. Readings in various books on magic and the occult had also stirred my thinking about geometric form. In magic rituals certain geometric shapes play an important part: the triangle, the circle, the square, the pentagram and the six-pointed star are deeply symbolic and considered beneficent for many reasons. I began to play with the idea that these forms were not only symbolically healing, but had actual power to heal and transform.

During this period I caught a cold and one evening found myself becoming seriously ill. I had a high fever, my throat was sore and very painful, all my muscles were aching. I was at a retreat in the woods and had nothing on hand to relieve the symptoms. (There were, no doubt, numerous herbs growing in the forest which would have helped, but at that time I knew nothing about herbal medicine.) I was lying in bed, feeling terrible, and wondering what I could do. My thoughts turned to geometric forms, and I decided to try an experiment. I visualized a white star (the pentagram had struck me as a particularly powerful symbol, and white felt clear and cleansing) above my head and then imagined it entering through the top of my head and settling in my throat. I went to sleep with this image strongly in mind, and when I woke up during the night (which was often as I was in a fevered, restless state) I returned to this image of the white star in my throat.

The next morning my fever was gone, as was the painful sensation in my throat. I still had a mild cold but was able to shake it quickly. I was stunned, however, by the fact that I was almost completely well. Familiarity with my own physical patterns had caused me to conclude that my condition the previous night was the turning point between being mildly sick and being very ill. But the unexpected had happened. It was as if I had condensed several days of healing into one night. I had taken no medicine, nor even made a suggestion that the star image should heal me. It had simply been an experiment in the healing power of geometric form.

I used this particular image in another instance, when a kink in my neck went unrelieved for some time and began to cause all the muscles on the right side of my back to knot. After several days, the pain began to be unbearable. One night I remembered the star image and decided to try another experiment. (The results of the first experiment had surprised me so much that I felt a little in awe of it and had done nothing more with it.) I entered a meditative state and began to image the white star turning rapidly and emitting a powerful ray in the painful area (like a "sparkler" one sees on the Fourth of July). The pain began diminishing rather quickly, and I felt a sensation of looseness in my neck, as if it were "unknotting." When the pain was entirely gone from my neck, I continued the treatment, imaging the star in all the central areas of tension in my back, feeling each place successively "letting go" and relaxing. Again, there was no suggestion that this image would heal me. The next day I was entirely well.

These were not controlled experiments. Several factors may have caused the healing process to occur. In the second instance the meditative state was no doubt a factor. But in the first instance I had not entered a meditative state. I went into the experiment cold, very much as one might dive into an unfamiliar body of water. Though suggestion was not used in either case, my evolving theory about geometric form made sense on a conscious level, and it is likely that belief in it was already there subconsciously. But I must emphasize that in both cases I did not have conscious expectations, one way or the other. What remains important for me is the fact that I did heal, and it has prompted me to feel that it is important that we research this area and discover what can be done, not only in treating the body, but in treating the psyche as well.

Uses of the Pyramid

For centuries people have been puzzling over the mystery of the pyramids. Now, as current research on the pyramid is published, we are beginning to understand that the pyramid is like a massive stone encyclopedia, a book of knowledge from which we can make astronomical calculations and measure natural cycles. For instance, the circuit of the base of the pyramid is 365,240 inches. Our terrestial year equals 365.24 days. The sum of the base diagonals of the pyramid is 25,826.5 inches. The procession of our equinox is 25,827 years.

The Frenchman M. Bovis was the first to discover that the shape of the pyramid holds one of its natural secrets. In exploring the Great Pyramid of Giza, he found dead cats and other small animals in the King's Chamber, who had apparently wandered into the pyramid and died of starvation. The strange factor about these dead animals was that there was no smell of decay to them. Upon examining the animals, Bovis found that they were dehydrated and mummified. He then built a small replica of the pyramid and oriented it to true north. A third of the way up (the King's Chamber is exactly in the center of the pyramid) inside the model, he placed a freshly dead cat. In a few days, the cat had mummified.

Further experiments with placing other organic materials inside the pyramid has shown that it definitely retards decay and spoilage. One obvious use of the pyramid, then, is as a natural refrigerator. An Italian milk company now puts their milk in pyramid shaped cartons. They have found that, in these cartons, milk keeps indefinitely without refrigeration. Not only will the pyramid keep food for long periods of time, it may make the food taste better. G. Patrick Flanagan, who has done a great deal of research on the pyramid, has developed an item he calls PEP, which is a Pyramid Energy Plate. He claims that the taste of cigarettes, coffee and alcoholic drinks is changed (improved) by the Pyramid Energy Plate. He did not present any material about changes in food items.

The Czechoslovakian experiments with the pyramid indicate that it is a cosmic generator which can actually re-group the molecular structure of inanimate objects. Karl Drbal, a Czech radio engineer, made further experiments after reading of Bovis' work with the pyramid. He placed a used razor blade inside a six inch high model of

Cheop's Pyramid and oriented the pyramid to true north. Drbal found that the blade recovered its original sharpness, and that the longevity of the blade was increased enormously by storing it in the pyramid. Drbal concluded that the environment of the pyramid had caused the crystals of the blade to return to their original form.

After reading of Drbal's experiments with the razor blade, I reasoned that if the shape of the pyramid had a corresponding effect on living organisms, it should be useful in renewing energy. I have been told of an elderly woman, who meditates in a pyramid twenty minutes a day, who reports that her wrinkles are disappearing.

Small pyramid structures can be purchased or built. They should be particularly useful for people who are exhausted or physically debilitated. Short periods of time spent resting or meditating in a pyramid will give you a concentrated sense of renewal. Patrick Flanagan reports that experts in the field of meditation say the pyramid increases the intensity of meditation. This may be why the ancient pyramids were used as sacred religious training or meditation chambers.

Those who wish to grow some of their own food may find it useful to construct the simple frame of a pyramid, cover this frame with ultraviolet transmitting plastic, and use the pyramid for a greenhouse. A few of these greenhouses have been built, but it is too early to know the results of this experimentation. It is reasonable to assume, based on other experiments with the pyramid, that such a greenhouse would produce strong, thriving plants, and may even increase their potential to provide nourishment and energy.

It may also be interesting to conduct experiments on the effects of the pyramid on dreams and fantasies. For those who feel need to contact the inner world, and have had trouble doing so in the past, the pyramid may be useful in stirring the impulse to dream and fantasize. One wonders, too, about the possible effects of the pyramid on the hypnotic state, and if hypnosis or self-hypnosis sessions conducted inside the pyramid might have greater depth or vividness. The effect of the pyramid on altered states is one which easily prompts speculation and should be researched thoroughly.

I was given the opportunity to experience the pyramid when a small one (six feet high) was provided by Pyra-meditation at a day-long gathering of people involved in various psychic, eastern, and occult disciplines and ex-plorations. This event was sponsored by Marin College in Kentfield, California, and was entitled Innerspace Day. The pyramid was a very simple affair, completely open, with its shape delineated by aluminum poles. In the center was a large pillow, and everyone was invited by George Cooper, who was representing Pyrameditation, to try it out. After nearly two years of interest in the pyramid, it was wonderful to find it really and readily available to me. I was not disappointed. A few moments after sitting in the center of the pyramid, I felt a current of energy above the top of my head, which then passed along the length of my spine. I then began to experience a sense of solidity, of being grounded, which I still find impossible to communicate verbally. The energy flow moved outward from my spine to the whole of my body, bringing with it a sense of radiant heat. I have felt these sensations before, in the state of meditation, but I was impressed by the intensity of the energy and that it took only a few minutes to bring on this sense of well-being and renewal.

After experiencing the pyramid, I look forward to the day when its benefits will be fully acknowledged and such small pyramids are made available wherever people work at long and concentrated tasks and need to replenish energy.

I also attribute to the experience of the pyramid a rather sudden yet thorough understanding of an abstract philosophical principle of t'ai chi ch'uan which I had known about but never really grasped. This has to do with the eight directions one faces while playing t'ai chi, and that part of its health-giving effects have to do with being in harmony with universal lines of energy. I had been thinking about the importance of the pyramid being oriented to true north, and that this had much to do with my sense of being in harmony with the cosmos while sitting in that space, when I suddenly realized that the Chinese had applied the same principle to the prescribed directions of t'ai chi ch'uan. (One always begins a round of t'ai chi by facing north.) This was not book knowledge or anything given by a teacher—it was that complete sense of knowing which we feel when, all at once, a door opens in the mind and we are "enlightened."

There is already much evidence that the pyramid has healing power. George Cooper of Pyrameditation tells me that people are daily relating to him amazing experiences with the pyramid. I quote only one letter that he has received, from a woman with a congenital deformity who had tried to find relief from her pain through numerous doctors, chiropractors, an acupuncturist and psychic healers.

> . . . . Since sitting under one of your Great Pyramid Frames, I lost all of the pain in my right shoulder and arm which I have suffered for years due to a congenital deformity of the spine and other bone structures. It was almost inconceivable to ever believe I could have complete freedom of pain, but I have. And I can thank you . . .[12]

Once a person has had contact with the pyramid, it is difficult to believe that it is not more readily available to, and made greater use of by, individuals and institutions. I am convinced that this amazing structure, preserved out of the past, will, in time, be an important part of our future.

The Dome and Other Structures

The Geodesic Dome is another remarkable structure, created in our own century by the genius of Buckminster Fuller. Although many building inspectors still look askance at the dome, it is actually more durable than the more normal rectangles people are used to living in. And though its unusual design presents challenging and complex problems for the dome dweller, I understand that dome dwelling can become a habit which some prefer not to give up.

I remember the deep pleasure and gratitude I felt the first time I traversed the spiral of Frank Lloyd Wright's Guggenheim Museum in New York City. For the first time in all my museum travels, I was not worn out by the architecture, but actually felt elated and energized by the space in which I was viewing works of art. How are we to know, unless we experience it, what effect it will have on us to dwell and work in a hexagon, a trapezoid, a sphere?

The actual construction of geometric spaces for healing requires research. The incredible pyramid, for example, is rendered useless unless it is oriented to true north. The materials used may also alter the effect of the geometric shape and its resonating quality. The amount and kind of light, the colors that are present, plant life and any other artifacts that are used—all these factors must be considered. But the first and most important step is to realize the tremendous potential inherent in different geometric structures, and the numerous ways in which they can facilitate the healing process. If we open ourselves to the concept that the *shape* of the space we dwell in can alter our state of being, then we can make the ancient and esoteric knowledge of geometric symbols, once only meant for a privileged few, available to help and heal many people.

The Symbolism of Numbers

The philosophical premise that underlies all Chinese medicine is that the universe is perfect and harmonious, and that the state of disease is one in which we are out of harmony with nature. The healthful state is one in which we experience a sense of harmony, of balance and equilibrium. No matter how a particular illness is diagnosed, certain states are commonly present (in various combinations of degree and kind) in those who are suffering mental and emotional distress. These states are excess, confusion, fragmentation and lifelessness. They are all ways in which we experience being unbalanced, or discordant. Geometric symbols, translated into structural design and image, can unlock doorways into the harmonious, healthful state. With these symbols, it becomes possible to modify excess, clarify what is confused, make whole what is fragmented, and renew what is lifeless.

In considering what is needed to aid the healing process, it will be helpful to have certain geometric symbols present as image—in the form of drawings, paintings, photographs, or in mobiles and sculptures. Their presence would then transmit, on a subconscious level, the ideas which these symbols contain.

In the book *In Search of the Miraculous*, G. I. Gurdjieff gives a lecture on symbolism, and on the symbology of numbers and their relation to geometric figures. He explains that one of the central ideas of objective knowledge is the idea of unity in everything, and that to transmit this idea (in a form which would transcend ordinary language) was one function of myths and symbols. Myths were designed to reach our higher emotional center, and symbols were destined to reach our higher thinking center. Gurdjieff then discusses the numbers two, three, four, five, and six, and the geometric symbols which express them: two parallel lines, the triangle, the square, the pentagram, and the Seal of Solomon, or six-pointed star. He states that these symbols "... possess a definite meaning in relation to the inner development of man; they show different stages on the path of man's self-perfection and of the growth of his being.[13]

Two expresses the way in which we normally perceive ourselves and the world around us—as a duality. All of our "... sensations, impressions, feelings, thoughts, are divided into positive and negative, useful and harmful, necessary and unnecessary, good and bad, pleasant and unpleasant."[14] In the state of duality, a person's life is largely mechanical and independent of will. One is controlled almost entirely by circumstances. In the realization of this mechanicalness and in the attempt to become conscious we begin to:

> ... set a *definite decision*, coming from conscious motives, against mechanical processes proceeding according to the laws of duality. The creation of a permanent third principle is ... the *transformation of the duality into the trinity.*
>
> Strengthening this decision ... gives a permanent line of results in time and is the *transformation of trinity into quaternity.*[15]

The next stage, the construction of the pentagram, has many meanings. The most important of these relates to what Gurdjieff describes as the "five centers" to be found in every human being: the thinking, the emotional, the moving, the instinctive, and the sex. Once the five centers are brought "into harmonious accord," we have locked the pentagram within us, and become physically perfect. It then becomes possible to express the six-pointed star, for, "... by becoming locked within a circle of life independent and complete in itself ..." we are "... isolated from foreign influences or accidental shocks . . ." and we embody the Seal of Solomon.[16] At this point we are in command of ourselves, we decree and master our own destiny, rather than being enslaved to fate.

Gurdjieff's explanation of the symbolism of numbers is an expression of unity in the universe, and of the potential wholeness in the human being. The circle, for instance, has for ages represented this idea of wholeness. Symbols, as Gurdjieff states so clearly, are a *synthesis* of knowledge, and they communicate that knowledge on a level other than the intellect. The person who is fragmented or confused may be helped by experiencing, or seeing, wholeness and clarity in structure and image. The idea of order in the universe might begin to permeate and bring her thoughts and feelings out of disorder. Excess can be modified by exposure to a system where balance is always present.

People who have difficulty carrying out plans, completing projects, who suffer from lack of organization or are never quite able to translate ideas into reality, may be helped by experiencing the square. In numerology (the science and study of the vibrations of numbers and how these vibrations affect us) four is the number of earth, of materiality and concrete work. It represents foundation, and the building blocks which turn ideas and visions into reality. The square is the symbol of solidity and permanence. Actually building something out of square panels or square stones and involvement with the weight of material objects will help to impress the meaning of the square in the mind.

A person who feels discordant, incomplete, afraid, or who needs a sense of integration, may be helped by experiencing the pentagram. The pentagram has become popular now as a stained glass design, and as such it may be used as a free-hanging object to contemplate. It would also be useful to build a two-dimensional pentagram which can be stepped into, to experience oneself as a pentagram. This position provides a sense of strength, wholeness, and solidity. Held for awhile, a feeling of mastery begins to invade the muscles and the mind. Perhaps it is mastery over ourselves, over a particular domain, perhaps over the universe.

The mantras of India, consisting of certain words and sounds, are said to produce a vibratory rate in the physical system which can actually change the body and emotional make-up of a person. This happens on a level other than the conscious one. It is an invisible process. Exposure to the geometric symbols in therapy is meant to have this kind of silent, subliminal effect. Translated into image, these numerical symbols will produce effects on a deeper strata—on the emotional, mental, and spiritual planes. They will serve to remind people of other states of being, and stir in them memories of wholeness.

IV

SOUND AND SILENCE

Today I can hear the birds which live in the trees beside my house, a cement drill about a block away, the almost-constant and slightly muffled sound of traffic, and the distant hum of a factory. This much sound input is average for most Americans, and even more is the norm. Our population is concentrated in large metropolitan areas where people are deluged by the noise of traffic, industry, machines, media, and the thousand and one sounds of other people going about their business and the daily act of living.

As human animals we have an incredible capacity to adapt to our environment and the conditions surrounding us. After three years of living in New York City I moved to the West Coast, and realized that a "shutdown" process had gone on inside me. It was the only thing that made it possible to survive the daily rape of my senses and sensibilities. My eyes and ears, my sense of smell and taste, had all contracted to a tremendous degree. My ears, in particular, had become somewhat numb in order to make the noise level bearable.

People need to experience areas where the sounds of civilization are absolutely minimized, and natural sounds abound. We need silence enough to hear the wind in the trees, rain on the roof, birds singing, water washing over stone. These sounds quiet our being, and enable us to better hear our own inner rhythm and the voice of wisdom and guidance that flows like a deep river beneath the more obvious, louder, and conflicted voices and identities we hear daily.

In the healing process, along with the effects of silence and natural sounds, we must remember the beneficial effects of music, both listening to and playing music. I once heard Seiji Ozawa, conductor of the San Francisco Symphony, compare the orchestra to the city park. The park, he said, is where one goes to see the trees and the sky, to watch children play and listen to the birds sing. We must have the park, for it is necessary to our spiritual renewal. And for the same reason, he felt, we must have an orchestra. We need music in our lives, for it is truly the language of the soul.

It is not within the scope of this work to cover the many uses of music in therapy or the details of how and when it should be used. There are many fine books on this subject, and there is an excellent summary of different therapeutic techniques in a chapter titled "The Healing Effects of Music" in Assagioli's book *Psychosynthesis*. From that chapter I wish to quote a passage written by Georges Duhamel, the French writer and surgeon. It is one of the most powerful statements I have ever read of the place music can have in helping us through times of crisis, suffering, and anguish. Duhamel is speaking of his experience during World War I, when he served as a military surgeon at the front:

> Whenever I happen to ponder upon music, upon the upliftments and clarifications I owe to it, upon the graces it has showered upon me, upon the secret relief for which I owe it an ever-lasting gratitude, and upon the place it occupies in my thoughts and even in my decisions, I often evoke certain days of the year 1915.
>
> During my hours of rest, in the evening, I drank deeply of the humble song I played on the flute. I was still very unskilled, but I kept at it, closing my lips tightly and measuring my breath . . . By and by my most painful thoughts went to sleep. My body, which had been completely occupied with the ef-

fort of enlivening the magic tube, became lost to thought. My soul, purged of its miseries, relieved, freed from all anguish, rose, lightly, in luminous serenity.

I began to grasp that music would permit me to live. It could certainly not diminish the horror of the massacre, the suffering, the agonies; yet it brought to me, at the very center of the carnage, a breath of divine remission, a principle of hope and salvation. For a man deprived of the consolation of faith, music was nevertheless a kind of faith, that is to say, something that upholds, reunites, revives, comforts. I was no longer forsaken. A voice had been given to me with which to call, to complain, to laud and to pray.[17]

We are still too much held in check and suffering the consequences of the Age of Reason and the Rule of Science. We tend to be too caught up in intellectual processes, in analysis, and in clinging to an objectivity which often becomes a sense of superiority to subjective experience. In creating a healing environment, we must remember our own wholeness, and the many aspects which compose our being. When we think of the whole person, there are so many levels, so many avenues of approach. We need to awaken not only the will to be well, but also the laughter in each of us, not only to clarify the sense of reason which enables us to bring order into our lives, but also to leave intact the touch of madness which lets us share in the splendor of living that children and gods know. Music moves the heart and soul; it is the source, the wellspring of enthusiasm which the *I Ching* speaks of so distinctly and beautifully:

When, at the beginning of summer, thunder— electrical energy—comes rushing forth from the earth again, and the first thunderstorm refreshes nature, a prolonged state of tension is resolved. Joy and relief make themselves felt. So too, music has

. . . there is much that can heal itself, if given time and space to heal. . .

power to ease tension within the heart and to loosen the grip of obscure emotions. The enthusiasm of the heart expresses itself involuntarily in a burst of song, in dance and rhythmic movements of the body. From immemorial times the inspiring effect of the invisible sound that moves all hearts, and draws them together, has mystified mankind.

Rulers have made use of this natural taste for music; they elevated and regulated it. Music was looked upon as something serious and holy, designed to purify the feelings of men. It fell to music to glorify the virtues of heroes and thus to construct a bridge to the world of the unseen.[18]

Sound and silence are ancient ways of healing. They feel forgotten in our modern world of medicine. We have known for centuries the effect that music can have on the hearer, yet it is seldom thought of as necessary to our health, or used as part of the healing process. We know what a deep sense of well-being and stillness can come over us when we escape to the silence, the gentler sounds of the country after a prolonged stay in the daily bombardment of noise in urban settings. But we do not use this knowledge as skillfully and completely as we might. To regain our health, and the health of the planet, we must more and more turn our attention to these simple, traditional, and ritualistic methods of healing. We must explore them anew and weave them well into our complete prescription for wholeness.

V

LIGHT AND LIFE

For the past few days, it has been foggy and cool in San Francisco. In a long stretch of that interior time which is intensive writing, I have mainly stayed indoors. This morning the fog dissolved and blue sky broke through. I had an irresistible urge to step outside, and was greeted by warm sun and the fragrant air of my neighbor's flowers. The dense, heavy time of summer in the city is waning. Autumn is approaching; one can sense it in the moisture of the air, the feel of the ocean in the wind, the quality of the light.

Before retiring last night I assigned my unconscious the task of working on the chapter on light. The world responded and the sun is casting a particularly brilliant light—clear, warm, and beneficent—a light that attracts me, and reminds me that I am a child of the sun.

We are all children of the sun, but a great many of us have forgotten it. The sun quickens life and sustains us. It is the central powerhouse which provides nourishment and warmth for the entire earth. We have no life without the sun.

The industrial age introduced an era when people and commerce moved indoors, after centuries of rural and wilderness life, in which a great deal of our activity took place outside, under natural light. Most people have adjusted to this transference and are hardly cognizant of the effect it may have on us to be indoors so much of the time, under artificial light, and cutting ourselves off from the sun even outside by wearing glasses, dark glasses, contacts, and being inside vehicles so much of the time.

I first became interested in the effects of artificial light when I started teaching t'ai chi ch'uan to college students. The classrooms on campus were all fluorescent-lit and cold, even sterile, in feeling. A great many rooms had no windows at all (not uncommon in the modern building) so that even daylight classes had to be conducted under the harsh neon light. I had never liked neon, and in reading of W. H. Bates and his work with vision I discovered that it can be a very poor source of lighting. Uncomfortable with the atmosphere, I decided to do something to change it, and the simplest, most immediate answer was to change the lighting. Bringing my own lamp (incandescent light) and many candles to class produced sufficient light and gave the whole atmosphere a softer, gentler, note—very much in keeping with the meditative feeling of t'ai chi.

This simple change was very effective. As people walked out of harsh, neon-lit rooms into this "t'ai chi environment" they became quieter and more relaxed. Softer lighting seemed to make people less self-conscious and more receptive. This change also produced a greater amount of interaction between students, and they began helping one another, rather than comparing themselves to each other. It is interesting that the change in lighting also marked a new sense of ease in teaching and communicating.

Health and Light, a book by John Ott, contains a wealth of information about light. Dr. Ott, a photobiologist specializing in time-lapse photography, was already interested in and working with the effects of light on plants when one day, he broke his glasses. He had for some time been suffering from arthritis, and had begun to use a cane to help relieve some of the weight from his hip; then his elbow began to give him trouble. He describes the pain and trouble this ailment caused, and the many treatment he had tried, prior to breaking his glasses.

The problem of what to do continued to become more acute; then, one day I broke my glasses. While waiting for a new pair to be made, I wore my spares. The nose piece was a little tight and bothered me, so I took them off most of the time. The weather had been nice for several days, and there was some light work outside that I did as best I could with my cane in one hand. Suddenly I didn't seem to need the cane. My elbow was fine and my hip was not bothering me much even though I hadn't taken any extra amount of aspirin. It was hard to figure out why my arthritis should suddenly be so much better. My hip hadn't felt this well for three or four years. I began walking back and forth on the driveway. Fifteen minutes went by, and I must have walked a mile. I ran into the house and up the stairs two at a time to tell my wife . . .[19]

Since the only difference in his lifestyle and activity at the time was the lack of glasses, Dr. Ott was convinced that the rapid improvement in his health was due to exposure to natural light without any covering over his eyes. He took a trip to Florida (where he had often been in hopes of relieving the arthritis, but to no avail) to bask in the sun without his glasses. "Before the week was up," he reports, "I played several rounds of golf on a short nine-hole course and went walking on the beach without my cane. I felt like a new person."[20]

This incident caused Dr. Ott to be very interested in the relationship between light and health. In his own life, he began spending as much time as possible outdoors, and moved his office from the basement to a corner of his plastic greenhouse. He wore his glasses as little as possible, and after six months a check-up revealed that he had to have a new prescription, as he no longer needed such strong lenses. An x-ray on his hip also revealed definite strengthening and improvement, with a complete disappearance of a thirty percent restriction of the rotation of the hip joint.

Dr. Ott states that a friend who tried his natural light regimen no longer suffered from hay fever. Another man, who had diabetes and suffered from severe attacks during a period when he was working on an assignment which required an intense amount of artificial light, had the blood vessels in the retina of both eyes burst. He became almost totally blind, and Dr. Ott notes that he always wore thick, strong glasses just before incurring the blindness. He continued to work for the same photo processing company—in the darkroom. When Dr. Ott reported his experience with arthritis, arrangements were made for this man to work outside as much as possible, and he also spent time at home, whenever he could, out in the light. Six months later he could distinguish different colors and was beginning to recover his sight.

Dr. Ott's continued work with light revealed interesting results, none of which he is willing to make absolute claims about, since he feels not enough research has been done. His findings are astonishing, and so much in keeping with principles of natural healing that I can only wonder at the "resistance" to Dr. Ott's ideas. At the beginning there was not much enthusiasm about his work from medical and scientific authorities. There is a great temptation to report to the reader a lengthy summation of Dr. Ott's findings, but I think it would be better to recommend his book to you, and outline some of the more immediate ways in which you can bring an awareness of light into your own health consciousness.

Find as much time as possible to be outdoors in the sunlight. Spending enormous quantities of time indoors under artificial light can be physically and psychologically detrimental.

If you wear glasses or contacts, develop a habit of spending time regularly in the sun without them. If you have worn them for a long time and find that the light hurts your eyes, you might begin with gradual doses. Never look into the sun directly. W. H. Bates, *Better*

Eyesight Without Glasses, offers excellent exercises, particularly gentle "sun-bathing" exercises for the eyes. If you are in the habit of wearing dark glasses while outside, you are still cutting yourself off from what you need in exposure to sunlight, since Dr. Ott's work indicates an intimate relationship between health and the full spectrum of the sun being able to reach the eye. (The full spectrum does not penetrate ordinary glass.) Try to strengthen your eyes by wearing dark glasses less frequently, and avoid pink-tinted or red-tinted glasses. Dr. Ott found that constant exposure to this particular ray (also in pink fluorescent light or psychedelic red light) increased irritability, hyper-aggressiveness, and negative states in general.

One of Dr. Ott's important discoveries in his work with both plants and people is that most fluorescent light, and glass, omits the ultraviolet ray of the spectrum. He thinks it very possible that we are "deficient" in this ray, and that it is necessary to our well-being. If you think of the spectrum of the sun as a complete food, then it is easy to see this deficiency. Fluorescent light has been developed which includes this ultraviolet ray, and it is also possible to wear glasses (both prescription glasses and sunglasses) which transmit this ray. Where you work, live, or learn, it would seem a good idea to install full spectrum lighting, and, if you must wear glasses, obtain full spectrum glasses. In his own life Dr. Ott has also, in many instances, replaced glass windows with ultraviolet transmitting plastic.

Two other interesting facts garnered from Dr. Ott's work—it was found that blue light (sunlight shining through blue plastic) reduced hostility and aggressiveness in minks until they became even gentle (which is not usual, as minks are normally handled with gloves). Speculation suggests that both natural light and blue-light therapy may be important in working with violence. In addition, Dr. Ott's research indicates that color television emits harmful rays which may affect our health and well-being. People who wish to try his light therapy are told to watch television as little as possible.

It is also possible that people who are ill or convalescing may be helped by increased doses of the ultraviolet ray, through the installation of an ultraviolet lamp. I would recommend that further contact be made with Dr. Ott (he is head of the Environmental Health and Light Institute at Sarasota, Florida) for intelligent use of this therapy.

Other incidents which Dr. Ott relates about treatment of cancer, incidence of leukemia, and other diseases indicate that light is extremely important in the healing process and may be so obvious that we are overlooking lack of natural light as a causative agent and its presence as a therapeutic agent, in a search for more complex remedies to go with complex diseases.

Individuals attempting to create for themselves a healing environment, should make every effort to become familiar with research in this area and establish an intelligent relationship with light, for light and life are synonymous.

VI

NOURISHING THE BODY

Food as Love

Everyone involved with natural healing or healthful living recognizes the importance of organic, wholesome foods in the healing process, and in maintaining good health. However, with food, as with other things, you must find your own way. Recent research at UC Berkeley has proven there is no "right" way of eating that works for all people. You are a unique being, with a unique chemical makeup and disposition. One should not force oneself into a mold, but rather discover what is natural and in harmony with one's own being.

Discovering what is natural is no easy task, especially in our society. Americans live in a synthetic, chemicalized, plasticized world, and we are deluged with advertisements telling us what we want and what's good for us. A great deal of what the media pushes at us is downright bad for the body. Most of the negative effects of these substances are not felt immediately, which adds to the insidious nature of the chemicals in our food. Certain diseases and illnesses caused by additives appear much later, even years later, and it becomes difficult to trace the origin of the illness.

Beatrice Trum Hunter's *Food Additives and Your Health* is loaded with facts. The book catalogues some of the more commonly found additives in our food (there are three to four thousand additives used in food, and most of them don't appear on the label). She tells us what these additives are, why they are used, and what effects they have on our health. Much of the research on these effects was carried on in other countries, where there seems to be greater concern with health than profit.

It seems absurd to be reading a directory of the poisons in our food. We cannot spend any more time accumulating evidence of *why* we need to change these conditions; it is too obvious. We can only survive if we put our energy into change, and into constructing alternatives. Yet Ms. Hunter's book needs to be read by thousands, perhaps millions, of Americans. It gave me fresh insight into why it is nearly impossible for me to walk into a supermarket these days. Her list of facts only confirms that on all the shelves, behind the pretty labels, hidden in the attractive packaging, is a wealth of poison—myriad avenues to destroying your health and well-being. Yet most people do shop in supermarkets, and most of them seem to be unconscious of the deplorable quality of the food they are buying. They believe what the food industry tells them so effectively through advertising, and they still think the FDA is there to protect them from "harmful substances" in their food. The FDA has bowed to pressure from the food industry in so many instances that they now remind me of a puppet presidency, still carrying the title of authority, while industry pulls the strings. And when the FDA attempts to make vitamins unavailable (except by prescription), bans certain healthful herbs, and makes it illegal to list the medicinal properties of herbs, all the while condoning toxins in our food, I really wonder who the FDA is working for, and what its purpose is. It is certainly not the servant of the consumer, and its intent can have little to do with our health. (My question about the FDA was recently answered by the book *Food for People, Not for Profit: A Sourcebook on the Food Crisis,* edited by Catherine Lerza and Michael Jacobson. This is truly a must-read book, if you want to understand the reasons for the general deterioration in the quality of our food, along with rising costs, and alternatives to the problem. It also clearly reveals the intimate relationship between top-level executives in the FDA and the Department of Agriculture, and the giant food corporations. In several instances the same men come from positions in the food industry into executive positions with the FDA and USDA—government agencies supposedly there to serve the public and protect the consumer—and then move back again into top positions in the food corporations.)

Even a small sampling of facts about the disturbances and illnesses—mental, emotional, and physical—caused by poor "food" can really shock people who are unaware of what is going on today in the name of feeding people. Some of these substances are so far away from the meaning of food as being something that nourishes and sustains the body they hardly deserve to be called food. Many other countries in the world, including Canada, will not import meat from America because it contains a growth hormone, DES—diethylstilbestrol—added to cattle feed because it reduces the amount of food cattle need to eat before they reach a marketable weight. DES has been proven carcinogenic. It has also been proven that many ranchers use an incredible array of waste products as roughage for cattle—ground up newsprint, sawdust, urea and styrofoam pellets, grain mixed with chicken litter or cattle excrement mixed with hay. This all gets passed on to you, the consumer. This is just a small sampling of facts, and only about one food substance, meat. Knowing what you are getting in packaged foods, such as desserts, instant foods, baked goods, candies, soft drinks, breakfast cereals, luncheon meats, snack foods, and the whole list of convenience foods, might cause you to stop eating. Immediately.

A man who read the same posted announcement about meat which I have reported to you expressed a wish that he hadn't read it, but said that it didn't really concern him. *Why not?* I wondered. He eats meat but is not concerned that it is loaded with substances which could cause illness and possibly be fatal. In part I think people like this man are not concerned because the condition of the inner organism is already in such a state of depletion they have lost the strength to protest. It is a case of a vicious cycle in which the disease expands itself, or the image of a cancer in which unhealthy tissue multiplies and consumes healthy tissue. Because we lack healthful food, we lose touch with our healthful impulses, and gradually lose the desire for health. This is particularly horrifying when you think of the number of children who are fed large quantities of sugar in so many foods, and imagine what their systems must be nourished on, and in what way that will affect their growth and direction.

Another interesting fact related to food is that—until recently—it was common for American physicians to go through their entire medical schooling without one course on nutrition. It is no wonder that so many of them are unaware of the relation of food to health, and that so many turn to drugs rather than correcting diet.

In Boston, Dr. Ann Wigmore, who is a naturopath, has two clinics where they are having phenomenal success in healing all kinds of serious diseases. Dr. Wigmore does not diagnose anyone. Her method of restoring health is to have people fast and allow the body to cleanse itself of toxins, then to give them concentrated quantities of wheatgrass (sprouted wheat) and raw foods which supply the body with all the natural energy it needs to heal itself. There are no stoves in Dr. Ann Wigmore's clinics. She has written a book about her work, called *Be Your Own Doctor.*

Other physicians who are aware of the relationship of food to health have found that many "mental patients" are simply suffering from wrong diet. Dr. William H. Philpott, who is assistant director of the Fuller Memorial Sanitorium in Massachusetts, has found that the underlying cause of seventy percent of all schizophrenia is an allergic response to certain foods, tobacco, or chemicals. High on the list of substances he eliminates from patients' diets are coffee, tea, sugar, alcohol, and tobacco.

In Europe, where they are a curing a lot of diseases which America still labels incurable, treatment generally consists of fasting to cleanse the body, and then a plentitude of light, raw foods, rich in minerals and vitamins. A very enlightening book, *Health Secrets from Europe*, by Paavo O. Airola, gives a complete description of different approaches to health in Europe—all of which stress *prevention*, rather than cure.

It is best to obtain food from people who grow organic fruits and vegetables, and from natural food stores where you can be assured of getting real food. In healing yourself, diet should consist mainly of simple foods—grains, fresh fruits and vegetables, sprouts, beans, yogurt, nuts, seeds, organic juices and herbal teas. It is also important that the atmosphere around the preparation, cooking, and eating of food be as pleasant and loving as possible. A good friend of mine is fond of saying that "Food is love." I quite agree with her. It is the equation that food is profit that has led us to the present depressing food picture in America.

Eliminating meat, or at least reducing the amount of meat that one eats, is very much a part of healthful living, not only for the individual, but for the earth as well. (*Diet for a Small Planet*, by Frances Moore Lappé, explains how and why the planet benefits from reducing concentrated amounts of meat in the diet.) Research in Europe and Russia has shown that meat induces and intensifies physical and emotional ailments. In Russia, for instance, a study showed that schizophrenics who had sugar and meat removed from their diet improved markedly, and when meat was re-introduced into the diet old symptoms showed up again. Meat is not included in any of the diets in *Health Secrets from Eu-*

rope, and all of these diets are designed to restore health.
Creating a daily diet that is compatible with you will
have to be determined by your own nature and good
common sense. In dealing with illness, however, it is
best to remember that meat is difficult to digest, and it is
generally better to draw your sustenance from light and
simple foods.

Every natural healing method I know is relatively
simple and inexpensive, if not actually free. What appears to be expensive (it costs more to buy food in a
natural foods store than a supermarket) is only the appearance of expense, since the harmful effects of continuing a more "economical" diet result later in
thousands and millions of dollars spent in hospital and
doctor bills, not to mention the psychic cost in terms of
suffering experienced by those who are ill or close to
illness. Yet in spite of the simplicity and low cost of
healthful living, most people persist in a disastrous way
of eating. Why?

First of all, many people are not educated about or
aware of alternatives. They go on doing what they've
always done or what they're told to do, because they
simply don't know that what they're doing is harmful.
And even if they get access to new information, they are
not necessarily given alternatives they can pursue to
change their ways.

People are also led to believe that they are doing the
right thing even though the information they are getting
is incomplete. People hear that whole wheat bread is
better for them than white bread. They go to the supermarket and very probably buy a version of wheat bread
which uses caramel to get the right color, still has pre-
servatives, and is puffed up and "vitamin enriched"
(which usually means that it doesn't have any nourishment value). These people think they are now eating
good bread, and they buy it because it is less expensive
than the whole-grain bread sitting on the same shelf. In

reality, they've done nothing for their health, only saved on their budget and given themselves an illusion of buying "better bread."

But given that you, personally, become aware of a need for change, are presented with an alternative, and shown how to pursue that alternative, will you make the change? Many people don't.

Most people I know say, and believe, that it is because they do not have the self-discipline they need to make that change. For instance, a person finds that fasting is a way to release toxins from the body, and wants to do a simple fast, perhaps drinking only organic juices for three days, or even one day. They find that it is easy to begin a fast, difficult to complete it. It is easy to get excited about a new way of eating, but difficult to carry it through until it becomes a natural way of eating. "I just don't have the discipline," they say. They often say the same thing about failing to carry out a program of exercise, or practicing a personal spiritual discipline.

Though discipline and will are involved to some degree in any process of change, I no longer think they are the important factors. Time and supportive space are the key. Discipline is not some externalized grit-your-teeth-and-do-it force. It comes from within, from the heart. Discipline is devotion to something you love, care about, are concerned with. Our present environment in America is constructed in such a way that healthful change in an individual's life is not only difficult, it is almost impossible. It requires more than discipline—it takes an Herculean effort. If you want to eat only organic, natural foods, you have to expend at least three times as much energy—and that is a very low estimate—as the person who is willing to just go to the local supermarket and buy what's available. This means it is in every way simpler, easier, and cheaper to buy chemicals instead of food. The food chains provide supportive space for poisons. And since that is what the food industry supports, that is what most people purchase. It is only one more example of the many ways in which this country pursues a suicidal course.

If you are attempting to make a change in your diet, whether it be for a few days, or for a long period of time, remember to provide supportive space for what you are doing. Keep photographs and pictures around you that remind you of the benefits of this way of eating. Read literature that inspires and motivates you. Write out your own description of why you are doing this and what you imagine will happen because of it, and then read your description often. If you live with other people, explain what you are doing and why it is important to you. Ask them for support, and discuss ways in which this support would feel real and good to all of you.

Since we are speaking of changing habits that have been acquired and developed over a long period of time, especially true with food, it is necessary to add the other ingredient—time. In the *I Ching* it is stated that only gradual change endures. People need time in a supportive space in order to change on a deep and meaningful level habits which may have been a part of them for years, or even a lifetime. After six weeks of being a vegetarian I did not have to discipline myself to choose a whole grain bread over white bread. My system demanded whole grain breads. I did not have to cut sugar out of my diet. My system couldn't abide sugar.

Given time and support, a healthful way of eating becomes a way of life, a part of one's self. The human organism is always ready to move in the direction of health, if only we will give it a little conscious help. I think it is still possible to reverse the present trend toward illness, if we will become aware and act, now. Not in the future, but today, we must begin the work of healing ourselves. An awareness of food as love, a return to wholesome, organic foods, is one of the most direct and most substantial ways that we bring about the healing environment.

Movement

Everyone knows that still water stagnates. And so do people, if they do not get enough exercise. Because of our cars, appliances, and convenience machines, most people who care about including exercise in their lives find that they have to redesign their time and activity. The major portion of jobs in this country are ones in which people sit indoors most of the day. Many people are used to this situation, and hardly think about the negative effects of convenience and "desk jobs."

Lack of proper exercise contributes greatly to illness. Authors Mike Samuels and Hal Bennett describe the reason for this in their excellent book, *The Well Body Book:*

> . . . . Because the unused muscle has less blood flowing to it, the cells which live in that area are more prone to infection, and they take longer to ward off disease, or to heal, than do muscles which are receiving a large flow of energy and blood.[21]

Real exercise is not just "busyness." Even if your day involves a lot of errands, rushing from one place to another, this is not likely to give you any sense of renewal. Movement should be renewing and energizing. The combination of elements that makes it so should be understood by everyone who desires good health.

Choose an exercise that you can really enjoy. Fresh air, deep breathing, and natural surroundings will all increase your enjoyment. Many people find that sharing exercise time with others makes it easier and more pleasurable. If you are not fond of heavy exercise, and you do like long discussions with friends, you might consider walking together while you talk. Taking time to move is taking time for your body—for yourself—in a very special way. If you've found an activity you like, it will renew and refresh you, and be a time that you truly look forward to each day.

Although there are numerous exercises to choose from, all of which can benefit you, there are a few things you should be aware of in any exercise program. Watch what you wear, especially on your feet. Check your clothing to be sure it does not constrict you in any way, and that the fabric "breathes" and allows your skin to breathe. Be sure you have good shoes. This becomes crucial if you take up an exercise like jogging, but it is important in your daily life too. My own experience, and that of others I know, has confirmed that a great deal of fatigue, tension, and aching muscles are caused by improper footwear. It is astounding what people do to their feet (and, consequently, the rest of their body) in the name of economy or fashion. And it is incredible that designers can produce some of today's footwear and not suffer some twinge of conscience at what they are doing to the human spine. The human foot is well designed, and the best way to walk is barefoot. If you must wear shoes (and most of us do a good deal of the time), choose a design which fits the natural shape and line of your foot, gives you a good arch support, and does not tilt your spine out of alignment.

It is well worth your time to expend some energy learning about the internal structure of the body. (I have listed a few books in the bibliography on this subject.) Not only will it give you a deepened appreciation of your physical being, it will help you to realize the importance of such things as good shoes, proper carriage, and ample exercise. For instance, many people do not know that we suffer a disadvantage because we walk on two legs, instead of four. The human being is constantly adjusting to the upright position, and the spine—the central axis and support of the body—needs knowledgeable help from you to maintain a healthy alignment. If you throw the spine out of alignment, or habitually carry yourself incorrectly, many other parts of the body are affected.

Muscles and bones must compensate constantly because of improper posture. The whole internal structure becomes weakened and invites aches, pains, and disease. The chiropractor is invaluable for adjusting the spine when a sudden movement or improper use of the body throws it out of alignment. But preventative medicine is knowing what the inner body is all about—it means carrying yourself well throughout the day, and learning how to walk, stand, sit, sleep, and transit to and from horizontal, sitting, and vertical positions. Good posture is not necessarily the set of rules you were given in school. It requires true knowledge about the internal structure of the body, and that knowledge can give you freedom and a sense of joy in every movement you make.

Exercise is another area in which the words discipline and self-discipline are often used. As I point out in the section on food, I believe that what is lacking for most people is not so much discipline, as it is supportive space. Most homes are crowded with people and/or furniture, so that it becomes difficult to do exercises which can be done indoors—yoga, t'ai chi, or dance. Large businesses provide lounge space for their employees (where people can sit and take a break from jobs in which they sit all day). People are not encouraged to walk together, or do simple exercises together (for which t'ai chi is ideal) as a way to refresh themselves or alleviate fatiguing schedules.

If you think that supportive space (or rather lack of it) may be part of the reason that you don't exercise, I recommend that you look around your own home, and see if you can set aside part of it for movement. Check your neighborhood or town for recreation facilities. Find people who are already involved with regular exercise—join a class, or check out your friends and family for movement-oriented people. Other people can be wonderful "supportive space."

Researchers in England have discovered that when you exercise a hormone is released in the body which is

connected with feeling "up" or happy. These researchers think the answer to depression is simply to exercise
every day for about ten minutes (at least) and to make it a
point to move when you start to feel low.

There's an odd thing about depression—it exerts a
downward force which makes it very hard to move, and
the more you succumb to depression the easier it is to
justify the depression and sink even deeper. The next
time you feel yourself getting depressed, play a game
with yourself: don't attempt to stop the on-flow of bad
feelings; simply add an activity. Tell yourself that it's all
right to be depressed, but that you have to move around
and breathe deeply while you think your depressing
thoughts. If possible, go outside to do this. Your perspective on the situation will change rapidly, even if the situation itself does not change.

For a long time Western civilization has placed great
reliance on mental energy. Many people think of the
head as the center of the body and the self, when in fact
your true body center is the pelvic area. There is a wide-
spread belief that mental activity is "important" and
physical activity is play—in other words, unimportant.
Done in the right spirit, physical activity is play. But
playing is as important as thinking. They belong together. Your thinking organ, the brain, is housed in a
body designed to move. If movement wasn't important,
we wouldn't need the body. In approaching health we
must always think in terms of wholeness and balance.
The whole of you needs loving attention, so remember
to move.

Massage

Massage is a healing art—a highly developed one in the
Orient and, thanks to the human potential movement,

beginning to be recognized as one in America. It is distressing that massage is still popularly vulgarized and debased, and that our lingering Victorian attitudes have kept massage from taking its rightful place in the healing process. Everyone needs massage, but particularly people who are ill or confined to their bed for long periods of time should regularly have a therapeutic massage. Jethro Kloss recommends massage for the treatment of many illnesses. Among other benefits, it helps to eliminate toxins from the body, and is wonderful for proper blood circulation.

Massage also puts people in a special state of mind, as it is a situation in which we can be totally receptive. As George Downing has said in his fine work, *The Massage Book*, massage is ". . . for anyone with whom you feel prepared to share an act of physical caring."[22] It is this caring which is transmitted from the person giving the massage to the person receiving it, and we respond to it not only physically, but on very deep levels of the psyche. In this relaxed state it is possible to touch center, and often possible to un-block energy in yourself which has been constricted for some time.

Since it improves circulation, induces relaxation, helps to eliminate toxins, and clarifies energy flow, massage is very important to the healing process, and can be of great value in any preventative program.

In the simplest attributes of nature there is power. Even dew shining on a spiderweb can remind us that there is meaning and purpose in life.

VII

AVENUES TO THE SUBCONSCIOUS

Image-Affirmation-Suggestion-Self-Hypnosis

There is an exquisite moment in the film *2,001* when the ape discovers that the bone which was only yesterday discarded as useless can become a weapon. It gives him power. As the ape experiences this moment of discovery, he throws the bone into the air, and the bone spinning in space becomes a spaceship. The magic of film is that it can condense centuries of evolution into a few seconds. In one moment you are witnessing the dawn of humanity and then, you close your eyes for a moment—barely taking time to blink—and you are looking at a new world. In the movies that kind of magic is acceptable. It is not only the wonder of film, it is the nature of it, the language of the medium. But when people are told they can produce this kind of magic in their own lives, and rather simply, they are reluctant to believe it. It is as if we have an inborn resistance to anything being too easy.

For many years I have been interested in the nature of change and expansion. How do we change? How do we learn? What causes that beautiful explosion in the mind when new circuits are connected and we suddenly find we are different, our life has changed, a door has opened to a new realm? I began to glimpse the incredible possibilities of the human mind the first time I was hypnotized. It was actually possible to feel as if I were floating in the air—a lovely feeling—and to experience the reality of another time (a peaceful scene from my childhood) as if it were happening now. And it happened simply by being receptive to a suggestion.

Although this first experience of hypnosis was pleasant, I didn't get involved with it at the time. I went on with my life as planned. Several years later, when I dropped out because I didn't like the way the plan was working, I had time to reflect, read, and wonder on how I might change myself and my life. It was during this period that I read *Psycho-Cybernetics* by Maxwell Maltz. Doctor Maltz, a plastic surgeon, became fascinated in the question of change after finding that some people who got a new face through surgery became new people—but others did not. Some people who were miserable because they thought themselves ugly, continued to be miserable after changing their external appearance. They still felt ugly inside. This led Maxwell Maltz to begin researching internal change.

I liked much of what Doctor Maltz had to say, and over the years I read a great many "self-help" books. I tried many of the techniques described, and found they worked if I persisted in using them. (Persistence and perseverance is crucial if you are interested in change, for the element of *time* is involved, so necessary to the process of change, and especially to change that endures.) After reading a book on self-hypnosis, I tried inducing the hypnotic state and found it was easy for me to do so. (Probably because I had had such a positive experience of it at first, I did not feel resistant to entering this other state of consciousness.) After becoming involved with self-hypnosis (particularly as a self-therapy method), I often juggled techniques, using myself as a kind of "change laboratory." It doesn't take long, in researching the area of avenues to the subconscious, to find that all the books basically say the same thing. The recurring theme in this process of internal change is that of imagination.

Image is the key in the area of influencing the subconscious mind. If you persist in repeating a mental picture of what you want, you'll get it. Most people participate in this process naturally (and unconsciously) by worrying. Worrying is repeating, verbally or visually, a series of negative pictures. If you take this process and project positive pictures (make positive your film, and your sound track), you get positive results.

Maxwell Maltz's basic explanation for this is that the mind works exactly like a computer (because the mind is the matrix of the computer), with the conscious mind acting as the programmer, and the subconscious mind acting as the computer. The computer has no choice but to manifest what it's been programmed to do. The way we program is by our thoughts—what we think, repeatedly say, believe, and particularly what we *image*. Everyone has heard the maxim that you are what you think. In metaphysics this is expressed as a law: energy follows thought.

Another important part of this approach to change is relaxation. The subconscious mind is most receptive when the conscious mind is relaxed. For this reason, it is highly recommended that you program the mind (through affirmation or image) in a relaxed state—either by inducing relaxation or utilizing naturally relaxed states, such as those moments just before you sleep or just as you are awakening. Hypnosis, of course, is a deeply relaxed state, which is why such phenomenal results can be produced with it.

One of the most important preliminary steps to any program of change is a realistic look at your present life. The use of image, affirmation, suggestion and self-hypnosis do not rely on will power. Through relaxation and conscious use of imagination an avenue is created which leads directly to the subconscious mind. The subconscious, once you begin to know it and communicate with it in this direct fashion, is a remarkable and stunningly honest aspect of the self. It is your own deeper self, with an amazing fund of wisdom; it is completely in charge of and responsible for all your physical and psychical functions. It is awesome to stop and reflect on the multi-dimensional process continuing in your body daily without your thinking about it. The subconscious is your personal memory bank where everything you have ever experienced is stored, and it is also your personal fabulous computer-genie, that sees to it that your goals are realized.

People often balk at this last image of the subconscious, because they think about all the goals they have, or have had, or constantly think on, without ever achieving them. Be assured that if you are true to those goals, they will be realized. Often without being aware of it, people have conflicting goals, a stronger image which takes precedence over the conscious goal. The subconscious can only respond to what you really believe about yourself and your life.

This is why I stress the truthful nature of the subconscious, and the need for a realistic appraisal of your life. Affirmation is not just repeating over and over again, "I am healthy, I am healthy, I am healthy." If your hair is falling out, or you can't sleep, or you often suffer attacks of anxiety, you are not healthy. If something is genuinely wrong in the system, the subconscious won't believe your affirmation. But perhaps you sincerely want good health. Then it would certainly believe your saying, "I want good health, I desire good health," and by repeating this you will have already triggered the mechanism in your subconscious which can manifest good health. In cases of healing in which one person affirms the health of another person when the other person is obviously ill, the healer is not just repeating an affirmative statement over and over again. The healer actually experiences the truth of the statement, by meditating on the divine perfection, unity, and wholeness of all creation.

One of the most amazing tales of self-healing I know concerns a friend of mine who contracted multiple sclerosis. The world kept getting darker and darker and one morning she discovered that she was blind. She recalls spending her day simply touching everything around her, loving every object, every thought, every aspect of her life. She spent her day in what she describes as "a state of adoration" for everything, for life itself. She saw everything as perfect in her life, *even the fact of her blindness.* She went to sleep that night with this sense of perfection pervading her being. When she woke up the next morning she had completely recovered her sight.

This state of perfection is a state of affirmation. It is a way to happiness, but only if you are sincere in seeing that perfection. Pause for a moment and look at your own life, particularly at those situations, conditions, or relationships that you consider a problem. Can you see those problems as perfect? In some way they are perfect because they are your problems; you created them and a basic intelligence in you weaves them into an invisible and benign pattern. If you can perceive your life, and especially your problems, in this way, you have opened the door to a solution. The solution is experiencing the harmonious, benign pattern underneath the complexities and difficulties of your "reality."

A realistic appraisal of your situation is also necessary because in order to change anything, you must first clearly state *what* you want to change, which is, of course, predicated by perceiving what needs to be changed. Once you can state the problem clearly to yourself, you can state the problem clearly to the subconscious, in the form of a positive suggestion, an affirmation, or a command.

Perhaps your problem is one of weakness in certain situations. You might state your suggestion like this: "I sincerely desire strength, courage, and self-command. I am discovering whatever I need to know in order to find this center of strength in myself." In doing this, be fully aware that you have the capacity to change weakness to strength, the *potential* for strength. You are simply awakening the potential, and activating that particular stream of energy.

And to effect the change you desire most rapidly, you would image the process as already *complete,* the answer found, the goal realized. If you can image it clearly enough to experience it, feeling and thinking as you would if you had already found your solution, then the goal is realized. You will find that the time span between imagined reality and the manifested reality is very short indeed. For the subconscious cannot tell the difference between imagined and actual experience. In explaining the imagination in *The Memory Book*, authors Harry Lorayne and Jerry Lucas present some evidence about the eye which reiterates this:

> . . . . Research carried out by the department of basic and visual science at the Southern California College of Optometry indicates that when you actually see something an electrical impulse reaches the vision center of the brain. They've also discovered (rediscovered scientifically, since ancient philosophers said the same thing) that there is not much physiological difference between the electrical signals that are activated by the mind's eye and ones that are activated by the eye itself.[23]

I am not including in this chapter any detailed explanation on the techniques of self-hypnosis, since there are many excellent books available, and I do not want to give a cursory view on a subject which is fascinating and deserves a thorough study.

One of the most important uses of hypnosis is regression. In a hypnotic state it is possible to regress to any time period, even back to birth, and so uncover source material for present beliefs, behavior, fears, and illnesses. Absolutely everything is recorded and stored in the unconscious, and through the avenue of hypnosis, we can tap this memory bank and relive an experience which we may have consciously forgotten, but which still affects and influences us. Once this material is brought into consciousness, it is available for an objective view, and we can determine what we want to do with that material, rather than have it (subconsciously) wielding power over us.

VIII

PATTERNS IN DEPTH

The Occult Sciences as Diagnostic Tools

At one time I was concerned about justifying the use of occult knowledge to the skeptics which still abound. Skepticism is healthy, and there is still a vast amount of research to be done. But the fact that we do not have all the parapsychological information decoded into scientific and technological terminology does not prove that the information we have is valueless or, as some extreme "rationalists" state, nonexistent. Much of the parapsychological experimentation in this country was still geared to proving that psychic energy *exists,* when the book *Psychic Discoveries Behind the Iron Curtain* made it popularly known that the Russian scientific community had moved on to researching what psychic energy is, and to finding ways to harness that energy and channel it to our benefit. If one makes any sort of honest attempt to look, the literature about, and evidence for, psychic phenomena is ample. Those who still need justification have either not bothered to research the matter, or else they are looking at it with a very biased, unscientific eye. In either case, the diehard skeptics must find their own way.

It is encouraging that Kipling was not altogether right. East and West can meet—the path of science and the path of religion can come together in a holistic field of understanding. This meeting is inevitable in a balanced and harmonious universe. Teilhard de Chardin expressed this powerfully in *The Phenomenon of Man,* when he speaks of the conjunction of science and religion:

To outward appearance, the modern world was born of an anti-religious movement; man becoming self-sufficient and reason supplanting belief. Our generation and the two that preceded it have heard little but talk of the conflict between science and faith; indeed it seemed a foregone conclusion that the former was destined to take the place of the latter.

But, as the tension is prolonged, the conflict visibly seems to need to be resolved in terms of an entirely different form of equilibrium—not in elimination, nor in duality, but in synthesis. After close on two centuries of passionate struggles, neither science nor faith has succeeded in discrediting its adversary. On the contrary, it becomes obvious that neither can develop normally without the other. And the reason is simple: the same life animates both. Neither in its impetus nor its achievement can science go to its limits without becoming tinged with mysticism and charged with faith . . . .

Religion and science are the two conjugated faces of one and the same complete act of knowledge—the only one which can embrace the past and future of evolution so as to contemplate, measure, and fulfill them.

In the mutual reinforcement of these two still opposed powers, in the conjunction of reason and mysticism, the human spirit is destined, by the very nature of its development, to find the uttermost degree of its penetration with the maxim of its vital force.[24]

I can add little to what de Chardin has so beautifully stated, except to say that the premises which are the foundation for the healing of our bodies, our minds and our environment are born of this union between science and faith. In alchemy, this *mysterium coniunctionis* produces the divine child, a child of light. In our world, where illness still composes so much of the darkness, it may produce the healing environment—a place of light.

In creating a personal healing environment, the occult sciences may be of value to you in understanding certain basic patterns and relationships. It is possible, for instance, to trace the reasons for a period of depression from an astrological horoscope. The underlying theory behind the occult sciences is called Cosmic Theory by chirognomist Fred Gettings:

> ... "Cosmic Theory"... has come down to us from remotest antiquity, and ... pervades all the ancient teaching such as alchemy, astrology and early medicine ....
>
> The theory behind Cosmic Relationships ... is rooted in an instinctive platonism centuries older than Plato. Its mainspring belief is that the material world is merely "the outward image and copy of a heavenly and spiritual pattern." The pattern of the whole is reflected lawfully in the pattern of each of its parts: the same laws which act in the universe, act in Man, and again, on a different scale of being, in the world of the atom. No one thing can be meaningful except in relation to its higher and lower functions, and because each is part of the whole, nothing can be without meaning.
>
> .... We have, through our present method of splitting up nature to investigate it, almost forgotten that a whole exists. We have lost sight of the wheeling cosmic system in our minute and specialist investigation of its fragments. In trying so disparately to understand with our intellect, we have lost the sense of wonder which went with ancient knowledge.[25]

The above is from Fred Getting's excellent work, *The Book of the Hand.* It is unfortunate that the occult sciences went through such a long period of debasement and vulgarization, and that in our present time they are still suffering the effects of popularization. So many of the fine minds which are in a position to make use of and gain from the knowledge which the occult sciences can impart are closed to them because of a previous prejudice. The attitude of Western science toward the occult sciences has been for a long time one of superiority and a rigid refusal to acknowledge their worth. On the other hand, the time of reawakening to these ancient sciences, which occultists predicted, has come about. It is good to see that a cross-current of communication is slowly beginning between our respected sciences, such as physics, biology, chemistry, and astronomy, and the ancient sciences of astrology, alchemy, chirognomy, and numerology. Recent acknowledgment by Western medicine of the wisdom of acupuncture is opening doors everywhere which have been closed for centuries. And the whole realm of exploration into our psychic faculties is the ground where the ancient and the new can meet to start a nucleus of integration which will benefit all of humanity.

The search to understand ourselves has been going on since consciousness began. Other ages before us have built astounding civilizations and achieved remarkable things. These ages which preceded us organized their knowledge and understanding of man in the universe into systems, and these systems are the occult sciences. Like any science, the occult sciences each have a vocabulary. They are languages which have been, for too long, foreign to us. It is important that we now begin to understand these languages and to use them skillfully.

Astrology:

The most important diagnostic tool we have from the occult sciences is the astrological horoscope. A random study of other occult sciences such as chirognomy (popularly known as palmistry), numerology, and alchemy quickly reveal that everything is based on and related to the cosmic pattern of the planets and the stars. Astrology is truly a thorough study of humankind. At a recent lecture given by Dane Rudhyar, who has done so much to relate astrology to Jungian depth psychology, he reminded listeners that the individual horoscope is an expression of the universe at a particular moment in time—and that each individual is the seed potential for that unique universal statement of being. It is inspiring to think of ourselves as a reflection of the cosmos, to be reminded, in the midst of the mundane and daily swirl of events, that we are also special, and that we have a destiny to live out and actualize. All this is in the astrological chart, including those conditions which are difficult or adverse, whether they be in the past or in the future. It can also reveal what is needed to bring the individual into balance, which personality traits and inner drives should be emphasized or minimized, what needs to be integrated and brought into conscious understanding.

There are many fine books of information on the horoscope. Suffice it to say here that the horoscope is a complete view of the individual—the conscious and unconscious life, the important cycles and major areas of concern, the basic drives and aspirations, the seed potential and the image of actualization.

Numerology:

Given a few facts, such as the name and birthdate of the individual, a competent numerologist can give a rather complete picture of a person in terms of the numerological structure of his life. This can deal with all the elements astrology covers, including the personality, the destiny, the important events in the past and future, the inherent nature of the individual, the work in which she is likely to find fulfillment, geographical locations where she is likely to find life harmonious or inharmonious, the numerical elements in her name which are either missing or are too heavily stressed in the structure of the personality. A numerological image of the individual is much like looking at the music of his life. We can see the dominant themes, and what is harmonious or discordant in his particular composition. Among other things, such a diagnosis might reveal symbolic work to be done with numbers, or geometric images and structures which might be useful.

Biorhythm, which is already a respected science in Europe and is beginning to gain some acknowledgment in America, is an offspring of numerology. It is a very accurate study of man's natural cycles and rhythms. A biorhythm chart can be invaluable in helping you plan activity in accordance with the cycle which will enhance that particular activity. For instance, certain cycles enhance physical activity, while others are more attuned to intellectual, or intuitive, work.)

Advance warning is also given of "critical days" when nothing major should be attempted.

Tarot:

In the hands of a skilled psychic, the Tarot deck can be a revelation on the inner life of the individual. Much work is also presently being done in using the Tarot as a tool of self-diagnosis. The Tarot is essentially a pictorial representation of archetypes and states of consciousness, and may be a rich source of material in uncovering what is needed in symbolic healing.

The formal Tarot deck is only one of the possibilities in the whole area of using archetypal image and fantasy as a means of discovering inner patterns. This approach to understanding the psychic life of the individual is a very important and exciting one.

Chirognomy:

The study of the hand as a means of understanding the whole person is still largely dominated by its popular connotations as a means of fortune-telling. It has been made intelligent use of, in some cases, by modern medicine and criminology.

A complete understanding of the hand requires a tremendous synthesis of knowledge. As Fred Gettings has pointed out, more than intellect is necessary: "It is well to remember that good palmistry is an art as well as a science, and the emotions can play just as important a role as the intellect."[26] In using chirognomy as a diagnostic tool, be certain of the competence of the individual palmist.

We can do much to elevate the quality and regulate the standards of palmistry by acknowledging its worth as a science and an art. It has been forced into a dark corner circumscribed by superstition, where people with some psychic talent but little spiritual character can prey upon our natural curiosity about our own character and destiny. The study of palmistry rightfully belongs in the open and frank atmosphere of the classroom, where it can be guided by competent and knowledgeable teachers. It should be used in the spirit and light of modern science, medicine, and psychology, where it can illuminate our understanding.

IX

DREAMS: CENTER AND SOUL

We know that sleep implies a certain therapy; that it is quite possible that in sleep, through dreams, things confused or obscured become clarified. . . . Thus, the door that leads into the world of sleep, leads into many mysteries, into strange paths and byways, about which we know comparatively little.

—Manly P. Hall
Studies in Dream Symbolism

Koestler . . . believes that the essence of discovery is the unlikely marriage of previously unrelated things . . . and the ultimate matchmaker is the Unconscious.

—Alan McGlashan
The Savage and Beautiful Country

The concept of the healing center was born long ago in ancient Greece. The Greek aesculapias—healing temples—were named after the physician and "patron saint" of medicine, Aesculapius. This legendary figure had three daughters—Hygeia (Health), Panacea (All-Healer), and Iaso (Healer). Aesculapius used dreams both for diagnosis and treatment, and in the healing temples named after him, dreams were the central mode of treatment.

The aesculapias were beautiful retreats where people went in times of illness or crisis, and at those crossroads in life when important decisions had to be made and there was a need to seek out greater wisdom. These temples were usually found near the ocean, set back in a grove of trees. Though some aesculapias were located in simple settings, the temple at Epidaurus, south of Corinth, became famous.

Upon entering the aesculapia, people would shed their own clothes and don the simple robes of the retreat. Here they stayed with priests dedicated to healing, and they often spent time in the company of artists (dance was highly valued as part of the ritual activity), until they felt ready to receive their answer. At the right time, the individual would go into complete seclusion and sleep. Healing would come in the form of a dream. The dream itself might be the healing agent, or else the symbols in the dream were translated by the priests into prescriptions. Some were fortunate enough to see the great Aesculapius himself in their dream. And at some temples the dream was the property of the priest: the individual would simply spend the night in the temple and sleep, and the priest would receive a dream in which the proper remedies were revealed.

There is now a considerable body of research on dreams which is available to the public. Although I am grateful for these revelations about the unconscious mind, I am also appreciative of the fact that, in an age when we are probing space and unraveling the atom into infinitesimal particles of energy, the dream remains one of the great and wonderful mysteries of human experience. Much light can be cast on our spiritual development by exploring and studying this mystery, and it may be that dreams are the protein, or essential building block, of actualizing selfhood.

It is imperative that we undertake, on a much more expanded basis, this work of studying dreams, for our technology is far ahead of our philosophical and spiritual understanding. Materially, we are in a unique position to extend this study of the self. I often think that we in the West, who have been so thoroughly engrossed for decades in the process of figuring out how to become completely comfortable, can now sit back, relax, and catch up with our ancient ancestors. While becoming technically superior, we lost much of the wisdom which enabled our "primitive" sisters and brothers to create sane, peaceful, and creatively rich societies.

One of the most stunning examples of such a society is the Senoi Tribe of the Malay Peninsula. In 1935 Dr. Kilton Stewart visited the Senoi, and found that there had been no violent crime or intercommunal conflict among these people for several centuries. Key to this peaceful and creative existence is the Senoi's under-standing of dreams. They encourage active participation in dreams and utilize dream messages and tools in wak-ing life. The dream is a central part of Senoi life, and the family shares, discusses, and works on dreams daily. From childhood on, Senoi people are taught to complete dreams, actively encounter dream enemies and demons, and to bring back from the dream world anything which might be useful, practically or artistically, to the com-munity. If, in the dream state, a person has a conflict with someone he knows in waking life, then the dream is presented to the person in question, and a resolution arrived at through the waking dream encounter. The Senoi are a truly astonishing people, and point the way for individual and interpersonal growth in our "more advanced" society. (I am sorely tempted to add a ques-tion mark to that phrase.)

Dreams have gone in and out of fashion in Western civilization. They have been revered, respected, dreaded, and laughed at. For quite a long period of time they were viewed as fanciful travels, hardly worth bothering over. In *The Interpretation of Dreams,* Freud brought them back into focus as an important source for understanding the unconscious. Jung brought fresh air and new light into the Freudian dream room, which is one in which dreams are mainly viewed as expressions of neurosis, repression, and infantile wishes. Jung stressed the importance of not forcing interpretations upon the dreamer, and felt that in dreams was the language of the creative and spiritual self, the path to individuation, and our link with the collective unconscious. More recently, Calvin Hall and Fritz Perls have both contributed immensely to dream interpretation, especially for the general public. Doctor Ann Faraday's book, *Dream Power,* is a very lucid and comprehensive presentation of dream research and interpretation. For people either beginning work on dreams, or wanting to deepen and extend work on dreams, her book is a clear and excellent guide.

For many years I have viewed dreams as soul food, the nourishment upon which the self is sustained. A short story by Truman Capote, "Master Misery" (in a collection called *Tree of Night*) illustrates this image in an evocative and haunting way. Master Misery is a man who buys dreams. For people who need money, it seems an easy way to get it. One has only to trek to his small office, tell him a dream, and be paid a small sum. But as the process goes on, the dreamer has a strange sense of being emptied, of having lost something which cannot be retrieved, and which made life human and holy. It is as if the person willing to peddle his dreams has, in reality, sold his soul.

Understanding our dreams, and activating that understanding in our waking lives, is essential to our health and growth. Working with dreams is potentially an important aspect of any healing process, but this work is too often neglected or avoided because of certain attitudes that block dream exploration. One of the biggest stumbling blocks is the view that the dream belongs to the high priest, that only the expert—the psychiatrist or trained therapist—is capable of unraveling the mysterious language of the unconscious. Remember that it is your unconscious, your territory, and your language. Though others may be skilled in helping you recover that language, the same skills are an inherent part of your own makeup, and ultimately, only you are capable of translating that language in a way which is meaningful and valuable to you.

In *Dream Power*, Doctor Faraday insists that dreams belong to the people who dream them, and that everyone is capable of understanding their own dreams. If you feel overwhelmed or deeply disturbed by your dreams, you should, of course, seek professional help. But as a general procedure we must take the dream out of that framework in which it is esoteric or abtruse, only to be dealt with by the expert. It is time for dreams to become a vital part of our living. Doctor Faraday states this clearly in her book when she says:

> . . . . unless people do begin to learn more about the inner springs of their behavior and to seek more authentic self-hood, it seems unlikely that the human race has much hope for any tolerable future at all. I believe this last part of the twentieth century is likely to be marked by all kinds of experiments in new ways of promoting self-understanding and emotional growth, and I am sure that the use of dreams has an enormous part to play in this.[27]

X

THE TRUE THERAPIST

Up to this point, little has been said about the traditional therapist because I am focusing on the idea of expanded therapy, where everything in the environment is potentially therapeutic. I do not mean to give the impression that I see no place for the traditional therapist in the healing process. When we embark on a long journey, it is preferable to have a guide, a friend, a reflector. A process of deep internal change is that kind of journey. Although there are people who have made it alone, or perhaps made it alone with the assistance of nature, or of music, or of a great creative work, we are fortunate when we have people willing to make the journey with us.

The healing process always involves some sort of harmonious relationship—if not with another person or a group of people, then with some aspect of the environment, or, to view it on an even more universal scale, some aspect of creation. Without this harmonious relationship healing does not take place, or is severely retarded. Recently I visited an osteopath for a treatment. I had seen this person about a year previously, and found her to be a true healer. She brought me physical surcease from pain, and put me very deeply in touch with myself. It was remarkable how simply, and lovingly, she had done this. During this first visit she had made time for me on a day when she did not usually see people, and the sense of slow, quiet time was very much part of this beautiful and rewarding experience. Because this person is gifted, she is very busy. When I went to see her a second time, I found that she had given up her normal day of rest completely in order to see patients and it was necessary to wait quite awhile to see her. She does not employ a secretary, so I answered her phone for her at least twice while waiting. I noticed from her appointment book that she was solidly scheduled for some time in the future and had been for some time past.

When I did go in to see her, she expressed some offhand irritability. Our time together I felt to be very short, and during it she seemed to be in a slightly negative place. Her irritability made me defensive, so we were in a mutually closed relationship. No healing took place during this visit; in fact I felt worse because of our offcenter contact. This experience confirmed for me that there is no healing without a healing relationship.

I once heard Suevo Brookin, who I consider a wise man, say, "Don't do things when you don't feel well. Don't try and take care of someone else when you don't feel well. If you're angry, don't even prepare bath water for a baby."[28] People who are ill, who are in physical or psychological pain, are just as vulnerable as a baby to angry or negative energy.

In working on yourself you may want someone to talk with, work with, be with. In seeking this kind of relationship, it is not uncommon to discover we may know a great many people, but only a few who will listen to us when we're down, or in need, or perplexed. There are fewer still who will do it regularly. What makes the work of the true therapist so difficult is the duration of energy that is required to see someone through their healing process to some measure of understanding, wholeness, and independence.

My own involvement and sense of kinship has been in the area of spiritual healing, in which it is possible to condense the period of healing into a very short period of time. I have great admiration for the therapist who travels with a person through what is always a rather lengthy process—stays with that person through her highs and lows, the mundane and the peak experiences—while she is attempting to understand and bring some sense of cohesion into her life. It is very difficult to do this skillfully, to remain alert, and to refrain from falling into the power traps that all healers and therapists are prey to.

The true therapist is a person who is willing to undergo the arduous inner journey with another, and who is also able to recognize his own human frailities and needs. Not only to recognize them, but make ample space for those needs. The school of therapy that one believes in is not nearly so important as the person transmitting the therapy. One's approach to healing is not nearly so essential as the compassion and skill of the person channeling the healing. There is nothing so important in the healing environment as human contact and the quality of that contact. Given the worst conditions and the most mechanistic structures, it is still possible for healing to take place if there is harmonious relationship between people.

XI

SPIRITUAL AND PSYCHIC HEALING

It is gratifying that the wave of interest in psychic phenomenon these past few years has produced such a formidable body of work: literature, films, and public assemblies where people have shared their questions, their research, and their discoveries.

There is now much evidence for the reality of psychic healing, including photographs of the human aura and of the energy passing between healer and receptor. There are several fine books that explain the underlying process of psychic healing in scientific and precise ways.

The subject of thought has also covered volumes. Authors who have been of particular help in understanding the nature of thought, and especially in its application in healing, are Joseph Weed (*Wisdom of the Mystic Masters*), Annie Besant, and C. W. Leadbeter (*Thought Power, Thought Forms*). A very complete discussion of thought, belief systems, and health can also be found in *Seth Speaks* and *The Nature of Personal Reality: A Seth Book*, both by Jane Roberts.

Almost everyone who describes thought likens it to a radio wave. Your own mind is the broadcasting center (and the receiving station), and when you think, the thought—a vibratory wave—radiates outward. This thought wave moves outward equally in all directions, continuing to emanate as long as the thought is held, but ceasing instantly when the thought changes or stops. These vibrations tend to reproduce themselves whenever possible, so that a thought you have on a certain subject is likely to arouse a similar thought in a receptive mind. Both distance and impact of thought upon the minds of others depend upon the clarity and strength of the originating thought.

In addition to creating a wave, thought also creates a *form*. The sea of energy in which we move is most responsive to thought, and it is as if thought uses this energy to clothe itself, and become embodied for a time in color and shape. Another image of the thought form is found in Robert A. Monroe's *Journeys Out of the Body*, in which Mister Monroe describes the absolute necessity for focused thought while traveling out of the body, for any idea passing through the mind instantly causes a response, creates a setting, or induces an encounter. The same thing is happening in this realm, but our bodies, due to weight and mass, prevent us from experiencing directly or immediately the effects of our thoughts. As we move more readily into different states of consciousness, and find our spiritual counterpart, it becomes easier and easier to experience the reality of the thought realm.

Even a brief introduction to thought radiation and thought forms can change the awareness of the individual. We see at once that we move constantly through an invisible ocean of thought, composed of our own and other's thought forms. This is a powerful environment which affects, perhaps more than anything else, our being and our behavior.

In creating a healing environment for yourself, and in particular creating this environment around family members and people you love, it is good to have a basic understanding of psychic healing. Psychic healing is contacting and channeling the superconscious energy which is the source and intelligent center of all life. Some people do this through meditation, others call it prayer, for some it is an act of imaging, or visualizing, a person as well and whole. Whatever the method, it is essentially a process of deeply concentrated thought coupled with elevated emotion, directed by a clear, strong, and intelligent will. Such healing is characterized by a spirit of humility and a sense of unity with all other beings; it is free of personal desire, pride, or ambition. Its focus is on giving energy to the self-healing process in the individual who is receiving the energy and allowing a deeper and higher intelligence to direct and guide that healing. Everyone is capable of channeling energy in this manner.

Although this book records several approaches to healing physical, mental, and emotional disturbances, the whole of this complex therapy can be reduced to just two vital ingredients: nutrition and prayer. By prayer I mean appeals to higher and deeper sources for help, guidance, and fulfillment. All healers, no matter what their particular technique or method of healing, speak of this intimate relationship with spirit. The foundation of healing is spiritual and depends on a full awareness of our dependence on the invisible intelligence which engenders life and brings cohesion to the whole universe.

The realization that this perpetual source of energy and wisdom exists makes all things possible. I have seen this wisdom manifested when praying for people in need, for the form which help takes is always one uniquely suited to the person who needs help. Concentrated and diligent prayer will unravel an answer to any problem, no matter how strange or difficult. The answer may come, and often does, in an unexpected way. But the solution is sure to present itself in time.

With proper nutrition, time, and prayer, nothing is beyond us. There are no incurable conditions, and no limitations.

If we care for those beings which are innocent and gentle, who are weaker than we, then the world is safe for all, and all are well.

PART THREE

THE HEALING CENTERS
OF THE FUTURE

"I am enthusiastic over humanity's extraordinary and sometimes very timely ingenuities. If you are in a shipwreck and all the boats are gone, a piano top bouyant enough to keep you afloat that comes along makes a fortuitous life preserver. But this is not to say that the best way to design a life preserver is in the form of a piano top. I think that we are clinging to a great many piano tops in accepting yesterday's fortuitous contrivings as constituting the only means for solving a given problem.

—Buckminster Fuller
Operating Manual for Spaceship Earth

I

THE COMPASSIONATE EYE

For some time I have been looking at those in hospitals, in institutions, at those who are vulnerable and weak. There is a multitude of beings—our children, our old people, our sick and our poor, the birds, the fish, the animals—all these suffer the misery the strong have created. In a world where survival of the fittest is the code, power survives. And if we live by this code, we will die by it.

Every day you can see small animals on the road that have met violent deaths because of our automobiles. These same cars cause poison to clog the air we breathe, and it sickens us. Who will speak for the air? Who will speak for the animals? Our rivers and streams are polluted by poisons from factories that spill waste into them daily. Our oceans are smeared by oil. Who will speak for the water, and for the fish that must live in this water? We raise trees to be slaughtered for a holiday we call Christmas. We have turned this holy day into a mass production, and the trees which cleanse our air and make breath possible are sacrificed on an alter of ignorance disguised as profit. Who will speak for the trees?

When beings gentler than ourselves begin to die, are imprisoned and neglected, then we can be certain that our own death is near at hand. If we care for those beings which are innocent and gentle, who are weaker than we, then the world is safe for all, and all are well.

II

THE PISCEAN INSTITUTION

Who's Crazy Here?

The term "mental illness" is of recent origin. It was coined by people who were humane in their inclinations and who wanted very much to raise the station of (and the public's sympathies toward) the psychologically disturbed from that of witches and "crazies" to one that was akin to the physically ill. And they were at least partially successful, for the treatment of the mentally ill *has* improved over the years. But while treatment has improved, it is doubtful that people really regard the mentally ill in the same way they view the physically ill. ... There is by now a host of evidence that attitudes toward the mentally ill are characterized by fear, hostility, aloofness, suspicion, and dread. The mentally ill are society's lepers.[29]

What does society do with lepers? Traditionally, they are hidden away in remote corners of the world—"out of sight, out of mind." The remote corners of America, where people are easily forgotten by society's "normal population," are its institutions—mental asylums, prisons, and, increasingly, hospitals. Although I see the healing center as a viable alternative to all these institutions, I am focusing in this chapter on one particular dinosaur of our time, the mental institution—described by psychologists Benjamin M. Braginsky and Dorothea D. Braginsky as "... dismal, gray, poorly ventilated, cavernous structures in which only madmen could reside."[30]

Our mental institutions are massive structures, and the support system that keeps them going, year after year, is extremely complex. At the heart of that support system is the belief that we need these institutions and that they do some good, if not in "curing" insanity, at least in keeping our "crazy people" off the street where they might harm others or themselves.

I have always had an instinctual mistrust of and dislike for institutions where people are incarcerated. As the evidence begins to accumulate about the ineffectiveness of our mental institutions, the lack of proper care for inmates in understaffed hospitals, and the now almost exclusive use of drugs in place of therapy, it becomes more and more difficult to understand why or how the public tolerates these institutions.

In gathering material to present a picture of the mental institution to the reader, I was struck by the findings revealed in two separate articles: "On Being Sane in Insane Places" by Doctor D. L. Rosenhan, and "Mental Hospitals as Resorts" by a brother-sister team, Doctor Benjamin M. Braginsky and Doctor Dorothea D. Braginsky. Though Doctor Rosehan's article is stressing the fact that mental health professionals cannot tell the difference between the sane and the insane, and the Braginskys are building a case for the use of institutions as retreats where rest is emphasized, there is an amazing correspondence in the data and conclusions of these people working independently of each other.

"On Being Sane in Insane Places" is an article about an experiment which was popularly tagged by the media as "The Insane Experiment." In this experiment, Doctor Rosenhan and eleven other pseudopatients (same people) applied for admission into mental hospitals in different parts of the country, were diagnosed insane, and admitted for various periods of time. The findings of this experiment are staggering, and the implications are grave. It clearly reveals that our methods of diagnosing insanity are ridiculous, that the diagnostic labels are in themselves damaging, and that the dispensing of drugs has all but replaced therapeutic methods. Doctor Rosenhan's description of the lack of human contact in these institutions, and the harshness of contact when it was present, is perhaps the most depressing aspect of his report.

> . . . . I have records of patients who were beaten by staff for the sin of having initiated verbal contact . . . . Occasionally, punishment meted out to patients for misdemeanors seemed so excessive that it could not be justified by the most radical interpretations of psychiatric canon . . . .
>
> Neither anecdotal nor "hard" data can convey the overwhelming sense of powerlessness which invades the individual as he is continually exposed to the depersonalization of the psychiatric hospital . . . . At times, depersonalization reached such proportions that pseudopatients had the sense that they were invisible, or at least unworthy of account . . . .[31]

Doctor Rosenhan also comments on the superior attitude we assume with such diagnostic labels as schizophrenia, manic depressive, etc., as if such labeling confirmed our knowledge, when in fact we still know so little about madness. Such bluffing, when it concerns human lives, is inexcusable. Yet it has been going on for decades. In reading Anais Nin's book, *The Novel of the Future*, I came across this description, recorded in the 1930's, of psychiatric diagnosis:

> . . . . In another section of the diary I found an exact reportage of a preliminary questioning of a schizophrenic man. Jean Carteret, who was interested in psychiatry, took me to a public psychiatric hospital, a sordid place where they tried to "classify" the form of insanity before placing the madman in an asylum. The blundering questioning

made a deep impression on me. Also the fact that
Jean and I understood the symbolism of the man's
fantasies, *whereas the doctor was merely using the
incoherence of them to prove his diagnosis . . . .*[32]
(Italics mine)

In both the Rosenhan and the Braginskys' articles, it
was pointed out that patients who had been coded and
classified into a "useless" category revealed themselves
as fairly effective and perceptive individuals, when
those having contact with them did not have precon-
ceived ideas (diagnostic labels) about their mentality.
Doctor Rosenhan reports that a great percentage of the
inmates in hospitals knew that the pseudopatients were
sane and had an idea of what they were doing there
(making a study). In no case were they told about the
pseudopatients. The patients simply observed their behavior. Members of the staff, who had ample opportunity
to observe the same behavior, never suspected that the
pseudopatients were sane. The staff saw them as being
what the diagnostic report said they were. As Doctor
Rosenhan points out, throughout the history of psychiatric canon:

> . . . the belief has been strong that patients pre-
> sent symptoms, that those symptoms can be
> categorized, and, implicitly, that the sane are dis-
> tinguishable from the insane. More recently . . . this
> belief has been questioned . . . . the view has grown
> that psychological categorization of mental illness is
> useless at best and downright harmful, misleading,
> and pejorative at worst. Psychiatric diagnoses, in
> this view, are in the minds of the observers and are
> not valid summaries of characteristics displayed by
> the observed.[33]

This view corresponds exactly with that of the
Braginsky's, who, in visiting different mental institu-

tions, expected to see abnormal behavior and subtle deviations from the "norm" of mainstream society.

> .... Instead, we found patients on the open wards who steadily performed demanding, complex jobs within the hospital, who lived cooperatively and peacefully with their fellow residents, and who participated in and led community activities.
>
> Yet year after year, diagnosticians labeled these effective human beings as chronic schizophrenics. To us it appeared that the deranged minds were to be found among the staff, who persisted in distorting reality in the face of overwhelming evidence to the contrary. By their own definition, the hospital staff was delusional.[34]

The Braginskys' report showed that most hospital inmates do not believe they are mentally ill or different from people outside of the hospital. They want to keep their civil and social rights, and do not feel that hospitalization should be grounds for divorce or bar them from re-employment at their former jobs.

But it is clear that the information the interviewers got from patients is not available to the hospital staff. It is not available because the staff does not even think to ask inmates questions about their civil and social rights. Staff members are interacting with a totally different person from the one that the Braginskys interviewed.

"The professionals cannot see, because between them and a clear view of their patient stands a conceptual wall."[35] The wall consists of three basic theoretical models: 1) the medical model, in which the patient has something akin to a physical disease, and drugs, doctors, and nurses are necessarily a part of the picture; 2) the behavioral model, which views insanity as maladaptive behavior which can be changed through behavior modification; and 3) the imprisonment model, in which the psychiatric inmate is the helpless victim of a sick society and the psychiatrist is his jailer.

One of the most unfortunate results of these theoretical models is that they are created by the "top echelon" of mental health professionals and their views filter down to the nurses and psychiatric aides, on to the public, and inevitably, to the patient. Doctor Rosenhan points out that, "A psychiatric label has a life and influence of its own." Once the patient acquires a diagnostic label it is expected that he will continue to manifest the same "abnormal" symptoms and behavior. "Such labels, conferred by mental health professionals, are as influential on the patient as they are on his relatives and friends, and it should not surprise anyone that the diagnosis acts on all of them as a self-fulfilling prophecy."[36]

These labels and the prejudices they foster also result in the lack of contact between inmates and staff which Doctor Rosenhan described. He reports that physicians, especially psychiatrists, were hardly available and seldom seen on the open wards. When patients and staff were in the same space, he found that there was very little real dialogue between them and an absence of simple eye contact on the part of the staff.

The Dinosaur Problem

By now most people have heard that we are, astrologically speaking, in a new era. We have left behind the Piscean Age, an age of faith, and entered the Aquarian Age, an age of knowledge. Aquarius is also the sign of the humanitarian, and it is not surprising that the reports made by Doctor Rosenhan and the Braginskys come to humane conclusions based on facts they observed, whereas the institutions they observed are dehumanized situations because of a system of belief.

I think of the mental institution as a dinosaur because it is like a giant, clumsy creature which is so obviously out of place in our present world. Yet it continues to exist because it is still fed by the people who believe it has a reason for being here. But the evidence clearly shows that we need a new approach to dealing with mental and emotional illness. Not only do we need a new approach we need a whole new way of thinking about what we have traditionally called "madness." Since there are so many people listed as emotionally ill in this country, it is no wonder that these people are thought of as problem members of our society. I do not think that they constitute the problem. The cause lies in the "normal world" which these people escape from and the real problem is in the dinosaur we provide to house them.

There is a wealth of new and vital knowledge which we are not currently employing to solve our dinosaur problem. We need only open ourselves to the possibility of change. A different perspective on the situation, and on our alternative, might reveal us to be like people stumbling in the shadows with kerosene lamps, insisting that this is the only way, when electricity is all around us, ready and waiting to be channeled.

What is the new approach? What are our alternatives? Doctor Rosenhan proposes part of the solution in speaking of the staff of the different mental institutions:

> . . . . It could be a mistake, and a very unfortunate one, to consider that what happened to us derived from malice or stupidity on the part of the staff. Quite the contrary, our overwhelming impression of them was of people who really cared, who were committed and who were uncommonly intelligent. Where they failed, as they sometimes did painfully, it would be more accurate to attribute these failures to the environment in which they, too, found themselves than to personal callousness. Their perceptions and behavior were controlled by the situation,

rather than being motivated by a malicious disposition. *In a more benign environment, one that was
less attached to global diagnosis, their behaviors
and judgments might have been more benign and
effective.*[37] (Italics mine)

Doctors Braginsky and Braginsky are also proposing
an alternative, perhaps more radical than Doctor
Rosenhan's, but only because it goes further along the
same line of reasoning. It seems to me that their proposal
is based on two main points made in their article. One is
that most mental patients are not crazy, for they are capable of adjusting their "craziness" to suit the situation
and fall in line with their needs. If threatened with dis-
charge when they wanted to stay in the hospital, patients
were able to convince psychiatrists that they were delu-
sional, anxious, and in need of more care. "When this
same portrayal would lead to the locked wards, they (the
patients) avoided it, presenting instead an image of
'healthy' mental patients."[38] In addition, the Braginsky
interviews revealed that what the patients considered
therapeutic was not the therapy sessions offered in the
hospital, but the opportunity to rest, relax, and socialize
in an atmosphere free of the responsibilities, pressures,
and ever-threatening violence and crime of our "normal" workaday world. The Braginskys present a picture
of the mental institution as the poor man's vacation spot,
where the price of admission is to act out insanity. My
own thinking on the alternative is so much in keeping
with the Braginskys' that I wish to quote at length from
the conclusion of their article:

> . . . . Our society provides opportunities for dig-
> nified withdrawal from the pressures of life in its
> resorts for the affluent, its retreats for the religious,
> and its communes for the collegiates. Some of the
> less affluent in need of escape have discovered the
> resort potential of the mental hospital. Casting them

back into society would not solve the problems that beset the ever-increasing number of surplus persons who are trapped in intolerable life situations.

We propose, instead, a "cooperative retreat" that might be a temporary refuge for some and a permanent residence for others but would destroy neither self-respect nor self-esteem. Life in this retreat would be conducive to personal renewal (not treatment) and refurbishment (not rehabilitation), whatever form that might take. Some persons might spend their time in meaningful work; others in athletic activities, informal socializing, rest and relaxation, while still others might see the retreat as a roof over their heads and three meals a day. The cooperative retreat would have no "degradation ceremonies," psychiatric management, or fences.

Although our proposal has moral and ethical implications, it comes not from ideology but from research. Psychiatric diagnoses, therapeutic programs, and mental institutions are moral enterprises that have little basis in reality. We should, therefore, discard them, thereby freeing the participants (and victims) from today's hypocrisy . . . . Society could stop misdirecting its energies and resources in the defense of a delusion.[39]

In the following chapter I present my own alternative, the healing center, and some of the experiences which influenced my concept of the center. I feel strongly that we must begin, as Doctor Rosenhan and the Braginskys have pointed out, by recognizing our own delusions about mental illness. In doing this, we can formulate a realistic approach to dealing with the problem. We can also become "part of the solution" instead of being part of the problem, and perhaps we can open a way to the healing process which our society and the earth we live on is so desperately in need of.

III

THE AQUARIAN ALTERNATIVE

Wealth is anti-entropy at a most exquisite degree of concentration . . . . we find that the physical constituent of wealth—energy—cannot decrease and that the metaphysical constituent—know-how—can only increase. This is to say that every time we use our wealth it increases.

. . . the most ideal is the most realistically practical . . .

—Buckminster Fuller
Operating Manual for Spaceship Earth

The Audacious Philosopher

When I began collecting material for this book I was a young, idealistic member of the humanistic psychology movement, and an aspiring therapist. During that time I saw that the humanistic psychologist, though much more open to different "paths" or "disciplines" of change and centering, was still rooted in a traditional mode of therapy. Therapy was mainly the exchange that took place between therapist and client when they sat in a room together and talked. Even group therapy struck me as being mainly a verbal and intellectual confrontation, expanded to include more than two people. It was then that I began noting the complex situations and relationships that brought on negative or inharmonious states, and in thinking of the healing process, I became excited about the infinite possibilities of using the total environment as a medium of healing, and the whole of a person's activity—mental, emotional, physical, and spiritual—as a process of positive change.

Pursuing work in my chosen profession and the daily involvement it engendered led me to discover that I am a philosopher more than a psychologist, a theoretician of therapy more than a therapist. It convinced me, however, that there are people who need and want the therapeutic relationship—essentially an involved, caring relationship between two people, one of whom is seeking, while the other guides (or at least attempts to guide) the seeking. I do not agree with the Braginskys that all therapeutic programs should be discarded, but feel they should be made accessible and available to those who want them, and should be considered a medium of change, rather than treatment. We must get beyond the notion of "fixing" or "curing" people. We can only offer help if a person really wants help, and that help must focus on the premise that all healing is self-healing, so that help really takes the form of showing people how they can help themselves.

We must also take an expanded view of therapy, and include the possibility of a natural therapeutic relationship, in which a person is seeking, while the other aspect of the relationship (not necessarily another person) guides, simply by its presence. A perfect example of this is in Herman Hesse's *Siddhartha*. Siddhartha, in his old age, becomes wise by dwelling and working on a river.

He finds the understanding and peace he sought all his life by watching the river, and being in relationship with it. In this kind of therapeutic relationship there are any number of possible partners—a tree, a plot of earth, a tool—are all potential ways to the answer a person is searching for.

Another discovery, made while working in a residential treatment center for "disturbed" adolescents, was that the institution was entirely dominated by the diagnostic model and the treatment-therapy mode. Not only does this have harmful effects, it produces a closed and narrow system. Although a "therapeutic program" might include various activities and confrontation-situations, the programs were basically fixed and rigid, for at the source of all these programs was the Treatment Theme—the dialogue between sick and well, sane and insane, normal and abnormal, and the endless dualistic games that are a natural result of this philosophy.

One instance of this rigidity was the subtle disapproval from older staff members when I sought a daily period of quiet during my shift (which was four days and three nights long) in which to do yoga. Since it wasn't part of the structured program, it was not to be included in the daily activity. This denial of a quiet interval which was for me centering and renewing made me feel that a staff member was something more than a person and should not, therefore, require a period of renewal. Observation led me to a different conclusion: I had to renew myself in their prescribed ways, just as the residents had to behave in the prescribed ways to get approval. Those staff-approved ways of taking breaks included sitting around and talking with other staff members, smoking cigarettes, drinking coffee, and lengthy reading of the newspaper. I did not smoke, couldn't stand the bad coffee, and reading the newspaper depressed me. The silence of yoga would have given me surcease from the constant verbal contact of the institution. Denied a personally satisfying way of refreshing body and mind, I went home massively drained after each shift and began to be sick more than during any other period in my adult life. Eventually I left this institution because the environment was harmful and solidly closed to change.

The decision to leave was made only after vigorous efforts to affect change. Finding the situation intolerable, in light of what I knew to be possible, I wrote a proposal for transitional alternatives. Younger members of the staff, if they had not already had similar ideas, were open to and excited about these alternatives. With only one exception, the administration was not so easily inspired. It was demoralizing to see that the more closed members of the staff, who were totally locked-in to the present system, were also the most likely candidates for future administrative heads.

Even though we are faced with people who believe in the present system so thoroughly that they are deaf to new possibilities, it is important that every single person who has recognized the need for change persist in presenting new ideas, voicing their opinions, and giving energy to intelligent alternatives. We must all be audacious, for our fate depends on our willingness and ability to enact change—now.

The Arrangement

In a film called *The Arrangement,* Kirk Douglas plays a very successful ad executive named Eddie who attempts to kill himself on the highway. During the long recovery period after his "accident," Eddie stops talking. His intense introspection leads him to relive scenes from his past, and to realize that he doesn't like the person he's become. When he does start talking again, he begins "acting out" in a way that causes everyone to doubt his sanity. When Eddie announces that he wants to give up all his property and material goods, and just "be," his wife declares him insane. But in all this internal and external upheaval (during which time he has not returned to work or any kind of normal schedule), Eddie begins to make peace with himself. At one point he declares, "I'm going away." When asked where he's going, Eddie replies (staring at his reflection in a windowpane), "Into myself." In solitude he begins a self-analysis, living out his childhood, replaying crucial scenes, saying things in the present which he was afraid to say in the past. When his wife and his lawyer finally get him to a mental institution, Eddie tells the doctor, "I want to stay here." It is easy to see why. For though Eddie had what appeared to be the perfect "arrangement"—perfect wife, perfect job, perfect home—his inner life and sense of self became distorted and finally forgotten in the midst of material success. His concern now is to work out who he really is and what he wants to be; he realizes that in the hospital he can do this uninterrupted by the cares and responsibilities of his "real" life.

This is fiction, but, as with all good fiction, there's a lot of truth in Eddie's story. It is not unusual for people who end up in mental hospitals to feel they have been living a lie. Dropping out of our reality may be the only way they have of recovering themselves. In the institution there is the possibility of rest, and in resting, the opportunity to find answers they were too busy to seek before.

There exists a "whole-making" energy within us. That which is whole within us, or the potential to be whole, produces an *actual* energy. It is this energy which splits the psyche apart when we have strayed too far from an inner truth. (In Eddie's case the drive to material success caused him to set aside the most cherished dream and ambition of his youth.) It is the same whole-making energy which we must trust in dealing with what we know as madness. How can we presume to cure that which by its very manifestation is already curing itself? The psyche has its own way, and we must, essentially, allow it time and space to mend itself.

If we acknowledge that the symptoms of madness are an expression of the system's drive to restore balance, we are in a better position to understand the nature of the mind. We can also see with greater clarity the qualities, beliefs, and values in the society which help to bring on madness.

Though we are not individually responsible for creating the present society, we are responsible for accepting and perpetuating the status quo. If poverty did not exist, would we have thieves? If the misery of the ghetto were not there, if people treated each other with fairness and love, could distortion be born?

In this sense we are responsible for those who are in mental institutions. We do not live in a sane society. People in mental institutions are there because they are unable to continue adapting themselves to the "American way of life." The American way of life has become an aberration. Look at what we accept. We package chemicals and trivia and call it food. We make lying attractive and glamorous and call it advertising. We "sell" politicians to the public and call it image-making. We drop bombs on other countries and call it pacification. Pollution, poverty, violence, crime, ignorance, hunger, and disease are all part of the American way of life. Any one of these factors, which we all live with every day, is enough to cause a breakdown. It becomes a matter of personal circumstance and sensitivity, then, as to who ends up in a state hospital with a label of "maladaptive behavior."

A Brief Vacation

Another film which brings to mind the need for an alternative is *A Brief Vacation*, Vittorio De Sica's final, and very beautiful, work. In this film, Florinda Bolkan plays Clara, a woman whose economic circumstances are completely the opposite of Eddie's in *The Arrangment*. Clara is poor—very poor—and she is the sole support of a family of four adults and three tiny children. Her family is almost parasitical, draining her psychically as well as physically. Every day she works at a grueling and terribly monotonous factory job. Though the film deals with the cure for Clara's physical disease, it is clear from the beginning that her mind and emotions are also suffering, for she is constantly angry, depressed, or in a dull state of half-existence.

Clara develops tuberculosis, and her "brief vacation" comes in the form of a prescribed trip to a sanitorium. Located in the mountains far from her city-smog ghetto "home," the sanitorium allows Clara the chance to experience the beauty of natural surroundings, clean air, an abundance of good food, and the opportunity to rest completely in spacious, private quarters. There is also a sense of gentle caring from the hospital staff, in contrast to the constant bickering and demands of her own family.

In this atmosphere, Clara becomes a different person. Not only does she manifest the radiant beauty of real health, she also discovers her natural intelligence, her ability to relate, to love, to reflect on the needs of others, and to contemplate the problems in the society.

Although many people in America who end up in hospitals with serious diseases are not as poor as Clara (and again, many are), their circumstances are similar in that disharmony exists on some level in their lives—in some way they are impoverished, and the psyche expresses this disharmony through the body, rather than through the mentality or the emotions. It is another way of signaling the person that something is wrong in the pattern of their life.

The sanitorium in *A Brief Vacation* has many of the

attributes the ideal healing center should have. What is lacking is that it only deals with Clara's immediate physical ailment. Once cured, she is sent home to the same circumstances, the same family, the same poverty, the same job—everything, and everyone, that caused her to be ill in the first place. She is sent home without counsel, without the chance to express her feelings about returning, without the opportunity to give voice to her new needs and aspirations (which in fact, the sanitorium has inspired and nourished), without, it seems, any awareness on the part of the staff of the difficulty in returning to her former life. At the end of the film it is impossible to imagine Clara able to tolerate her former circumstances, for she is now aware of her potential, and she has glimpsed the possibility of a richer, happier life.

In providing an alternative for people with physical and/or emotional problems, we must learn the causes, the source of those problems and provide the necessary counsel and "follow-through" energy to help people deal with the environment that has fostered the disease. It is not enough to give people a brief vacation. We must do everything possible to help people extend and expand the healing environment.

The Alternative

If we accept as a fact that our society is not sane, then there is no point in continuing to establish and maintain institutions that force people to conform to old, unhealthy life habits. Compulsory adaptation to our present mode of society is not the answer. The only course we can undertake is change—radical change. The concept of the healing center, total environments designed to restore health and a sense of balance, and to provide an education in harmonious relationship with the environment, would be an expression of radical change. It would also establish an intelligent alternative to our present institutions.

Explained simply, the healing center would be a gathering of people and a complex of dwelling and working spaces set in a rural area. It is most certainly the "cooperative refuge" that the Braginskys have proposed, but it will go further in that it will be designed to engender and support the change of consciousness which we must foster if we are to heal ourselves, our society, and, in fact, the earth itself. The center must be a place where the approach to healing and health is holistic. Rather than treat symptoms or analyze parts, the *whole* person will be considered, and help, healing, and nourishment will be offered from the whole of the environment. In the process of helping people regain their health, the center will also offer an education in preventative medicine.

Every individual who can realize a sense of wholeness, centeredness, and true health naturally multiplies our chances of bringing about a sane society. The healing center will be a microcosm—a small, sane society—where the embryo of a new world can be cared for, nourished, and strengthened. The strength people achieve in this setting, and the knowledge they attain, can in turn be shared and applied to their future and to those close to them, to the society and to the environment.

In concept and realization, these centers will make intelligent use of new knowledge we have concerning the healing effects of structural design, color, sound, light, and plant life. Great attention will be given to the importance of organic, wholesome foods in regaining and maintaining good health. Centers will grow their own organic food and establish a complete recycling system.

These centers must be staffed with strong, loving,

knowledgeable people. Staff members may be involved with natural healing, the human potential movement, or various spiritual disciplines. Centers will need people who are trained and can work with others in the area of dreams, movement, body awareness, massage, bioenergetics, psychosynthesis, transactional analysis, gestalt, yoga, t'ai chi ch'uan, meditation, psychodrama, and self-hypnosis—to name only a few. There are any number of approaches to health and healing which are valid. Various approaches can be integrated into a system which is uniquely suited to the needs of the people who reside at a particular center. It is, however, imperative that these approaches be humanistic, rather than behavioral.

There is also the possibility of including on the staff of the healing center psychic and spiritual healers, shamans, and people involved in the occult sciences, such as astrology, who can share their knowledge within the humanistic framework for those who wish to explore these areas.

The healing center will be practical in that people who stay there can learn how to live on the earth without polluting or pillaging it. They will learn to live in harmony with the earth and other species of the earth. There will be exposure to people who are organic gardeners and herbalists, people who understand the relationship between nutrition and health, carpenters who can teach others how to build simple structures and dwellings, those who know about alternative energy systems, such as solar power, and craftspeople who can instruct residents in their particular craft.

I will throughout this work refer to people who are entering healing centers as residents. To describe them as patients or define them strictly as the mentally ill or the emotionally disturbed is restrictive, and exasperating. These definitions have become too loaded. It is very much like trying to discuss the question, "What is real?"

Everything is relative. The people who are responsible for the administration of a healing center will be referred to as staff.

These centers must also include, work with, and nourish our higher consciousness—our spiritual self. An integral part of the healing center is recognition of the philosophy that this spiritual self does exist, a philosophy in keeping with Roberto Assagioli's school of Psychosynthesis:

> What distinguishes psychosynthesis from any other attempts at psychological understanding is the position that we take as to the existence of a spiritual Self and of a superconscious, which are as basic as the instinctive energies discribed so well by Freud. We consider that the spiritual is as basic as the material part of man. We are not attempting to force upon psychology a philosophical, theological or metaphysical position, but essentially we include within the study of psychological facts all those which may be related to the higher urges within man which tend to make him grow towards greater realizations of his spiritual essence. Our position affirms that all the superior manifestations of the human psyche, such as creative imagination, intuition, aspiration, genius are facts which are as real and as important as are the conditioned reflexes, and therefore are susceptible to research and treatment just as scientifically as conditioned reflexes.[40]

Much of this work is concerned with, and suggests the use of occult knowledge. As more and more of this "hidden" knowledge is brought into the light of modern scientific research and experimentation, it must be acknowledged that the ancients and the mystics knew more than the respectable scientific community has been giving them credit for. This occult knowledge now comes under the heading of parapsychology—the study of psychic energy, or psi, as the Russians term it. A great deal of our present parapsychological research is a process of deciphering knowledge which has been available to us for centuries, and translating that knowledge into a mode which the Western mind can see and accept. That mode is technology.

To say that we are in a technological age is, perhaps, another way of saying that we are in the Aquarian Age. Since the change from the Age of Pisces to the Age of Aquarius is essentially a change from an age of faith to one of knowledge, the Aquarian must know and grasp with her mind what the Piscean believed and accepted in his heart. Our technological exploration of meditation is an example. The effects of meditation can be felt and seen by anyone who practices it. However, a verbal description compounds the mystery to many people. But when the state of consciousness which is the meditative state is translated into alpha and theta waves on an EEG chart, we have a way of approaching the modern mind—a way of clarifying the mystery. In short, we make the invisible, visible.

The healing center will not be technologically oriented, but should make use of technology where it has proven effective in revealing to people their own self-healing capacities, such as with biofeedback mechanisms. It is my hope that the healing center as an alternative will be a culturally rich environment, expressing respect for, and making use of, many different healing traditions.

Healing centers may also function as retreats which can *prevent* breakdowns. Used in this manner, they would be places where people could go in states of exhaustion or crisis, when a period of quiet is needed to make difficult decisions, or to make room for the inner life to the exclusion of external affairs. I envision healing centers as part of a society which understands and respects that everyone has different cycles—that each of us at times feels the need to move in as well as out. We must be generous to ourselves, as the artist is, and make space in the structuring of our lives for that which is holy, mad, and mysterious.

All Life Forever

The last decade has brought on a revolution of consciousness. People of vision, like Buckminster Fuller, have made us aware that we have all we need to live successfully on this planet. But for that awareness to be complete and to begin to manifest in different social structures, we need to leave behind the concepts of scarcity, and survival of the fittest. They are obsolete. There is enough for all, if only we will make intelligent use of what has been given. Buckminster Fuller stated this succinctly: "If we do not comprehend and realize our potential ability to support all life forever we are cosmically bankrupt."[41]

In looking at the kind of environment which can heal people, we are inevitably forced to confront the environment which causes disease. There are still too many ghettos, too many people who are hungry, poor, sick— too many for whom the words "equal opportunity" are a cruel joke. And there are also those who have won their share of material goods and still find life meaningless— the taste of their acquisitions turning to ashes in their mouths. In short, the planet is crowded with people who are motivated by what Abraham Maslow has termed deficiency needs. This cannot change until we expend the necessary energy to change it.

In discussing alternatives we must necessarily discuss the funding of such alternatives. If one were to take as a comparison what we are spending in our present institutions as opposed to the cost of healing centers once they are in operation, the comparison would undoubtedly be in favor of the latter. Beginning costs are perhaps the biggest obstacle. However, this can be overcome in any of at least three ways, and perhaps the goal will be realized only through a combination of the three.

Even though it is the least likely of the three to come to fruition in the immediate future, government funding is one possibility. Through individuals voicing their desires to their legislators, it would be possible to gain support from the government with the funds, hopefully, administered in conjunction with the Environmental Protection Agency. Since healing centers will be communities based on an intelligent, harmonious existence with the environment, making good use of land and space, while in the same act expressing respect for the land, these centers will be a natural and positive expression of protecting the environment. While there is a great need for "cure" action, such as passing laws which make pollution prohibitive, there is an even greater need for "preventative" action, such as the establishing of healing centers. Certainly it is the right, and in fact the duty, of all citizens to express themselves to their government in this regard.

The second possibility for support would be from foundations or in the form of grants from large business corporations. Many organizations which employ large numbers of employees already have physicians and psychologists on their staffs. Some of the more progressive business administrators have made corporate investments in land where personnel and their families can vacation and enjoy leisure activities at lower than normal cost and, in some instances, without cost. Through these activities, concern for the whole person including the relationship and well-being of the family, is expressed, and it is within the realm of possibility that this could be expanded to include healing centers. Through the companies' group insurance plans, savings might be further realized by way of preventative care.

Two companies currently provide space on the premises where employees can grow their own gardens. These are cared for during planned breaks in the work day. Not only does this provide an opportunity for the employee to spend time in the sun and fresh air, it is also an encouraging step toward natural foods.

The third and certainly most viable and immediate possibility in making healing centers a reality is through individuals who believe strongly in such a system joining together to create groups dedicated to the establishment of healing centers. Once some headway has been made in this direction, funding from government, private corporations, and foundations will be more accessible. (A more detailed discussion of where and how to start individually toward making the healing center a reality will be found in Part Four.)

Whatever the source of funding, it is imperative that the cost of indigent people be planned for, since they are likely to need the healing center most of all. Here again, the ultimate savings, both in dollars and quality of human life, will prove worthwhile over the long run.

Our present reality reveals a government willing to make vast expenditures on defense and warfare, and a society ruled by its drive to monetary power. Comparatively little is spent on health, education, or the exploration of humankind's rich and creative spirit. Wherever we see poverty in its myriad forms, we see monuments to the tragic waste of human potential. We need to reorient and redirect our energy if we are to bring an end to that waste. Along with the women and men of genius, we must each realize our own capacity to change and to engender a better life on this planet.

IV

THE HUMAN TOUCH

Medicine must always be accompanied by prayer and good thoughts.

—The Book of the Hopi

During a talk I gave some time ago on healing environments, a person in the audience asked if I had a model of health. I could only reply that I knew what a healthy condition felt like for me, and that there seemed to be a reasonable degree of agreement between people on how they feel when they are sick. One definition of health which I fully agree with and which allows for a wide latitude of individual differences was recently given by Suevo Brookin, teacher and herbalist: "Health is a state of balance and a conscious way of doing things."[42]

I have no model of "normalcy" either. I agree with the philosophy that as long as you're not harming others or imposing your way on others, as long as you can respect my right to live life as I see fit, then what you do is okay by me. I don't want to impose my view of health on anyone. Everyone has to find their own *approach* to health. We are individuals, with individual needs and a unique way of doing and perceiving.

In presenting the concept of the healing center, the same allowance must be made for individual preference. Though I have a deep belief in healing centers and their potential, I do not necessarily feel that everyone will want to experience them, or respond to them positively if they do go through the experience. Perhaps some people prefer hospitals. If that is the case, they most certainly should avail themselves of hospitals when they

We must explore anew. . . these simple, traditional, and ritualistic methods of healing. . . and weave them well into our complete prescription for wholeness.

are ill. Many people, like myself, want an alternative to hospitals. No matter what our ailment, we can only heal in that setting where we are comfortable, where we can place our trust in the people who are administering healing and our belief in the way healing is administered. That is why it is so important to understand and be in touch with the effect environment has upon the healing process, and actively seek out, or create, an environment which will aid that process.

Fainting and Finding

Recently, I visited a friend in the hospital. Shortly after seeing her, I fainted. It is not an uncommon experience for me to feel faint in hospital settings. I had grown so familiar with the symptoms that I knew the preventative procedure by heart. But this time, on my way to the door to get some air, I tripped over a mechanism near the bed and in the next moment I had hit the floor and blacked out. The most serious consequence of this event was a decision on my part to uncover the cause of my feeling faint in hospitals.

That decision brought on a flood of response from my unconscious. I began to see that one source of tension and conflict in myself was in the inability to express negative feelings. During my second visit to the hospital, while waiting in the hallway, I felt the symptoms come on again. I was dizzy, my breathing was shallow, my sense of balance was slipping away. I sat down and began to concentrate on my breathing, praying to know what was going on inside me. I heard a voice in myself pressing, demanding that something be said. I let that voice go and found myself articulating, quietly and repeatedly, "I hate hospitals. I hate hospitals. I hate hospitals." This statement released a tremendous flow of energy. I saw clearly that I was overwhelmed by the sense of pain and fear all around me, and nearly traumatized by the mechanicalness of response to those who are ill. In *The Nature of Personal Reality* by Jane Roberts, this is what Seth has to say about our hospitals:

It seems that you are highly civilized people because you put your ill into hospitals where they can be cared for. What you do, of course, is to isolate a group of people who are filled with negative beliefs about illness.

Stimuli pertaining to health is effectively blocked in such organizations. . . . This isolation would be unfortunate enough without the application of drugs meant to help, but often given without understanding. Loved ones are permitted to visit the sick on but certain occasions, so those who wish them well in the strongest terms, who are closest to them and who love them, are efficiently prevented from exerting any natural constructive behavior.

For all practical purposes the ill are put into prison. They are forced to concentrate upon their condition. All of this applies quite apart from any other dehumanizing effects, such as overcrowded conditions, the denial of human privacy, and often the negation of dignity.

The individual is made to feel powerless, at the mercy of doctors or nurses who often do not have the time or energy to be personable . . . Furthermore, the natural elements of sun, air, and earth are refused him . . .

You are a part of your environment. . . . The sun makes you smile. The smiling of itself activates pleasant memories, neurological connections, hormonal workings. It reminds you of your creaturehood.

The old witch doctors operated within the surroundings of nature, utilizing its great healing ability, directing its practical and symbolic qualities in a creative fashion[43]. . . ."

Although I want not to negate the good that is done, I am outraged at how much more could be done that is now ignored. The institutions which dispense medicine, whether it be for physical or psychological illnesses, are still dominated by the old models and trapped in rigid and incomplete knowledge which has become dogma. And it is the patients who suffer the consequences of that rigidity.

In realizing what was causing shock to my system in hospitals, I found a center of compassion in myself. In touching that compassion I felt my longing for the kind of consciousness that can turn that emotion into knowledge of how to heal. I rededicated myself to the task, for I know it will take duration of energy to help bring about the changes I want to see happen.

Those changes are intimately connected with the changes that happen in the healers of our society. We are not in the habit of speaking of the "healing arts," but prefer to call them the helping professions. The word professional implies a degree of quality, skill, and thoroughness of knowledge. But there is a deeper level of love and commitment in the act of healing which makes it an art. These are Erich Fromm's words on the art of loving:

> . . . if one wants to become a master in any art, one's whole life must be devoted to it, or at least related to it. One's whole person becomes an instrument in the practice of the art, and must be kept fit, according to the specific functions it has to fulfill. . .[44]

Just as we cannot take a fragmented approach to diagnosing or treating a person who enters a healing center, so we cannot separate what is done in a healing center from those who are doing it. Centers cannot harbor the attitude of superiority which Doctor Rosenhan has found prevalent in our present institutions. The people who staff the centers must be a special breed of being. Knowledge is not enough. There must be a high degree of compassion, commitment, and consciousness.

Compassion, Commitment and Consciousness

Given the above qualities in its staff members, there must also be a basic working structure, designed by the staff of the healing center, which will insure the protection and growth of these qualities. Even the most well-meaning people, in institutions which are basically born of good intentions, can erode the compassion and clarity of staff members by not being aware of the particular problems and difficulties involved in the helping or healing professions.

It has been a standard saying for some time that the only way to tell the difference between the inmates and the staff of an institution is by who's carrying the keys. Along with the carrying of the keys goes a dangerous set of assumptions that can easily burden the staff and eventually undermine the whole working structure of the center. These assumptions read something like:

"I'm well, they're sick."

"I've got it together, they're falling apart."

"They need to work—I've done my work."

"My relationships and my ways of relating are clear—their relationships are muddy."

"I am always honest and if I'm not there's a good reason for it. They are seldom honest and when they lie it's because they're sick and afraid."

"I'm straight—they need straightening."

In a healing center these assumptions might extend to:

"I am spiritually whole and clear—they must be prayed for."

"I'm strong, they need to rest."

It would be easy to go on ad infinitum, but I think the message is clear. All these assumptions have a basic underlying theme: "Because I am staff, I am privileged—psychologically, physically, and spiritually I am beyond the work and the rest that it is right and good to demand of inmates, patients, and residents." I do not think these assumptions are conscious. Most often they are subliminal, and people act on them without ever knowing the motivating factors behind their behavior. Sometimes these assumptions are made for the staff by an administration which is removed from the actual working scene, and staff members are helplessly caught in an emotional atmosphere which they do not necessarily agree with but which, nevertheless, dominates them. The result of these assumptions is to eventually drain the staff members, which means it is impossible for them to be clear in the way they work with and relate to others.

How are these pitfalls to be avoided in the healing center? We must begin by remembering that the staff of a healing center is its core. It must be healthy and honest and growing, for from the core all the rest emerges. The basic assumption must be that no one is actualized—everyone is always actualizing their potential; this makes change possible, and a flow of new ideas, new approaches, possible.

The healing center embodies the concept of an ideal setting. Yet it must be understood that work in a healing center will be difficult and challenging. Though it is an ideal and beautiful setting, into the center will come people who are in depleted, negative conditions. To deal with these intensely negative states, day after day, in an effective way, staff members must be very much in touch with their own needs and their own ways of replenishing.

Recommendations and Suggestions
to and for the Staff

Basic Nourishment:

The food the staff eats should be the same food the residents will be eating, and this should be the finest organic food available. Staff should pay particular attention not to neglect meals because of pressure, and to have easily available high protein, high energy snacks. The present picture in our modern institutions, in which cigarettes and coffee (usually cheap, made incorrectly, and left to stand for hours on end) are the most easily available oral diversions, is so ludicrous that it is hard to believe. However, it is the reality that dominates most institutions and I stress this very basic need because people cannot function well, or for very long, unless they eat well. It may initially be more expensive to furnish bowls filled with nuts, raisins, and sunflower seeds, but the return in good energy will more than justify the expense. It will also be important for staff to remember, when sitting down to meals, that cares, problems, and duties must be temporarily set aside, or else no real nourishment can take place. Only in an atmosphere of calm enjoyment can the digestive system work properly to provide the body with what it needs.

Rest:

Work shifts will be scheduled according to the needs of the center involved. I imagine that many of the people who work at a center will also live there. Whatever the case, some shifts will involve spending nights on duty or on call. These shifts must be worked out according to individual needs. No matter how long a work shift is, the center must take care to allow within each shift enough time for sleep and rest. Attention should be given to different rhythms. Some people enjoy being up late and getting up late. Others feel most alert in the early morning hours and prefer to get to bed early. Though it may not always be possible to give everyone "ideal" hours, it is important that these individual needs be listened to and met as closely as possible. If not, it will affect not only the rest cycle of individuals, but also their dream cycles. A prolonged period of time away from habitual rest periods and time to dream can have a severely negative effect. Staff members may grow irritable, despondent, and depressed—not because of the work, but because of lack of sleep and time for the psyche to mend what was undone during the day.

In addition to sleep and dream time, there should be opportunities within each day to break from work. There must be channels for play and lighthearted activity. At regular intervals staff should take long rests and be completely removed from the setting in which they work. If work in a healing center is to be a labor of love, attention must be given to the natural cycles and needs of all staff members.

Another form of rest is in taking time out for movement. Ideally, centers should have two periods in the day set aside for activity such as yoga, t'ai chi, dance, or swimming. One of these periods should be at midmorning, another in the late afternoon. These are both periods when people need a "refresher." At least one hour a day should be spent in such activity for all staff members. It would be wise to finish such an hour with a few minutes of meditation or silence.

Clear Relationships:

There must be a basic sense of relatedness and empathy between staff members, and working structures should be set up so that exchange and interchange between staff members stays open and honest. The staff members of a healing center will come from a variety of disciplines, and all of them may not have a background in basic ground rules for "keeping the air clear." So it will be necessary to have a strong and simple outline that serves as a guide.

As much as possible, people should deal with difficult situations and uncomfortable feelings *in the moment.* Dealt with immediately, it is almost always possible to clear up misunderstandings.

Because situations do occur which need more time, or a better time, space must be made for staff members to talk together and listen to one another daily. If a situation seems very tangled emotionally, these discussions should be monitored by an objective person. There should also be a regular group-encounter situation for staff members in which they can, as a whole, look at all the different parts of the gestalt, work out problems, express likes and dislikes, voice current concerns, give one another support, and applaud positive inner and outer events.

There should be space for everyone to present their ideas and problems, their dreams and difficulties. This may include creating rituals which allow people to express all the deeply felt events in their lives. The ritual of sharing dreams and acting them out, with others partaking in the living dream, is one of the best ways to weave a true closeness between people, and to experience a sense of universality and common humanity. Another is to "dance out" one's demons and allies with each other. Often the act of taking a feeling, whether it be positive or negative, and translating it into an archetype, makes it possible to express what seems stilted, or even unimportant, in mundane terms.

Although it certainly should not be expected, and must be left to the discretion of individuals, it is probably good to encourage staff to occasionally meet outside of the working situation, so they can share their other realms and other interests.

No one, no matter what their position on the staff, should be exempt from this "clear relatedness" structure. As long as people are interacting daily, they need to abide by, and be part of, the guidelines which keep that exchange honest and free-flowing.

The concept of the healing center, with its spiritual base and projected images of people meditating together, might seem to make all this unnecessary. However, healing centers will still be made up of people, not saints, and problems are bound to arise. This is especially true because of the difficulties involved in dealing with sick and troubled people daily. If the staff does not take care to keep clear and alive the lines of communication and communion between themselves, it will eventually disrupt and undermine the whole community.

Individual Growth:

It will be important for staff members to be people who are in touch with their own inner lives and that which brings fullness and balance to their living. We all have our own ways, and in this day and age whole catalogs are available which list growth-expansion disciplines and paths. One thing that seems important is a periodic sojourn away from one's place of work—not just to vacation—but perhaps to study or to temporarily work in another setting and/or another field. In this way people can return to the center fresh, with a new perspective on their own way of life and their own way of working.

Whatever the source of funding for a healing center, a large portion of the budget should specifically be for salaries to support those who work, day after day, helping others. People are sometimes astounded by the high prices therapists charge, but it must be remembered that the task of the therapist is one of the most difficult, demanding jobs one could imagine. The gratification of seeing someone change, become a happier human being, is only there occasionally. The work involved in experiencing this "high" is usually long and arduous. Daily the therapist puts herself in the position of dealing with people's problems, with their depression and confusion. He must often risk their dislike and anger in order to be honest in reporting what he sees. She must find ways to remain clear in the midst of the emotional maze that people present to her every day. This is exhausting work. If, as is the case in too many institutions, the therapist or counselor must also be wondering how he is going to pay his bills this month, he will not last long. I think this "low budget for people" has a great deal to do with the high turnover of counselors in different institutions and clinical settings. It is not just nor wise to ask human beings to expend so much energy in their work and expect them to stay with it if they are not paid well.

The attitude of the administration in a healing center should be that of wise and loving parents, watching always to see how the family can grow, providing the best of nourishment, giving ample psychic and material support. This kind of intelligent support from the administration will release positive energy in staff members, allowing them to give fully to the residents who are in need. It will increase the possibility of long-term positions and relationships, thereby giving to the center a strong foundation consisting of people who know each other and their place of work well. In this way, a solid, healthy root system can be established in the center which will, in time, produce beautiful and lasting results.

V

OTHER CONSIDERATIONS

Environment in Relation to Violence

Violent people cannot be housed in healing centers, for it is a place where people go voluntarily, and there are no fences, or locked places. It is possible, however, to apply the principles of the healing environment in creating a setting for violent people. Much more research and work has to be done in the area of creating an alternative to prisons. For those who work in prisons, and particularly those who deal with violence, I would like to offer some suggestions, based on the model of the healing center. I am aware that this is a simplified picture of what can and must be done. I think it would be a good beginning.

Although I am not certain what kind of geometric structure is best suited to house violent people, this area is important, and we should not accept the rectangle or the square as the best or only possibility. Instinct tells me that curves and circular shapes can help to calm deep levels of anger and negativity. Clothes and shoes worn by residents should be simple, soft, and in cool colors—white, light blue, violet, or a tone of pale green, in which there is a higher mixture of yellow than blue. No meat, sugar, coffee or dyed teas should be served. Diet should consist mainly of simple, organic foods, fruit and vegetable juices, and herbal teas. Every means should be used to eliminate toxins from the body, including fasting, raw foods, saunas, massage, and heavy exercise. As much as possible, activity should be scheduled outside in the sunlight and fresh air. Start gardens, and have residents participate in real, useful work. Whenever possible, discover positive or creative urges in the resident and see if there is a way to direct

and give expression to these urges. A concentrated program of therapy must be available, so that residents can
contact the underlying causes of their urge to violence,
and in understanding these causes, can possibly begin to
dissolve rigid areas of negative energy. Work with
dreams will be very important.

Those who staff these centers for violent people
should be highly trained in martial arts such as akido or
t'ai chi ch'uan, which are entirely defensive arts in nature, and designed to "de-fuse" aggression rather than
oppose it. These arts also cherish life in all forms, and
people who practice them are taught how to confront
violence without harming the opponent, or at least harming him as little as possible. Practitioners of these arts
can tire out, rather than injure an opponent. These staff
members would be peaceful in themselves, centered in
their own strength and have no need to prove their
strength. This kind of staff would eliminate fear of residents from the atmosphere.

Attacks of violence, rather than be repressed with
drugs, should be housed where they can be given expression. Circular, padded rooms should be provided
where a resident can scream, throw things, and hit objects. In addition, color therapy can be used, by regular
exposure to blue light and violet light. If possible, involve residents in physical, meditative disciplines, such
as yoga.

Ritual of Transition:
Entering the Healing Center

The resident is leaving behind the external world and
entering a special environment in which people believe
in health as a natural condition, in wholeness as possible, and in which they are joined in the will to work
toward helping the resident to achieve this wholeness.
This ritual, however simple, should definitely establish
in the mind of the resident that he is now a member of

this community, and a part of the process which makes up the daily life of the community.

In addition, certain information about and concerning the resident will help to clarify the work to be done while at the center. Though this procedure might traditionally be called the diagnosis, it will not be for the purpose of "labeling" a resident. Diagnostic labels which are commonly used in the mental institution will not be heard or made use of in the healing center.

The entry procedure will be, instead, a kind of complete check-up. A record will be made of the physical and psychic condition of the resident. A self-statement made by the resident reporting how he feels and why he has come to the center will be requested. From these records, it will be possible to recommend activity while at the center and a basic healing approach. I would like to outline this procedure as simply as possible.

Complete History:

A complete history of the resident should be taken, including all that is known of the circumstances of her life, economic conditions, and physical and familial history. I must stress here that this should not become the kind of boring and exasperating record of information which we are already too familiar with in our present institutions. People must not be put through the frustration and humiliation of being left in pain, whether it be psychological or physical, until their history is "filable." No procedure in a healing center should become more important than the dignity of the individual, whether that individual be a staff member or a resident.

Physical Examination:

The physical examination should record the basic condition of the physical organism and reveal anything that is out of alignment or imbalanced in the body. From this diagnosis should come specific recommendations for diet, rest, and exercise. Since disturbances in the psychic life of the individual are always reflected in the body, it may be possible to clear up some problem areas by treating the body. Osteopaths and chiropractors may be needed. The insights, recommendations, and services of staff members who mainly deal in systems of therapy for the body will be called upon—such as people who work in bioenergetics polarity, massage, t'ai chi, yoga, and dance.

Psychic Diagnosis:

It is time that we employed the special talents of the gifted psychics among us. The psychic seer can report the state of the aura of the resident, and the state of balance, or imbalance, in the chakras (psychic centers) of the individual. This may often reveal, in a more direct way than the traditional interview, the predominant areas of conflict and disturbance in the individual, and the true nature of his emotional life. This kind of diagnosis may indicate certain physical exercises which are needed, or bring to light a prescription for color therapy. (This kind of diagnosis can certainly employ to advantage Kirlian photography.) Very probably the diagnosis will indicate what work needs to be done for spiritual synthesis to take place, such as work on the will, or exercises in concentration, meditation, and imagination.

Psychological Set:

There are already many traditional methods of diagnosing the individual to reveal psychological set and philosophical orientation. The kind of method used is largely dependent on the particular bent of the therapist involved. Where these traditional methods are considered valuable, they should be used. The kinds of psychological patterns which the occult sciences can reveal to us should be remembered and included. It may not be necessary to have on the staff of a healing center a representative from each of the occult sciences. This will probably not be possible, and in any case much of the information which such diagnosticians could give us would overlap.

Integration:

After all the diagnostic material is available, a meeting of the staff members involved in helping the resident should be held. Each should make a complete report and give individual recommendations. All the information must be compiled and organized into an integrated healing approach. There should be one person, or a team of no more than three people, responsible for organizing the diagnosis and prescription into a cognizant whole. This person, or these people, should also be responsible for keeping abreast of the current condition of the resident, and for making changes as they deem necessary and wise.

Clarity of communication between staff members, and between staff and residents, is crucial. Constant communication between staff members will minimize the negative effects of specialization. The right hand must know what the left hand is doing. And at all times we must refer back to the resident herself as the central and important figure in all this activity. The kind of breakdown which may necessitate residence in a healing center already indicates that the psyche is demanding attention and reintegration. If we know how to listen and can stay in touch, the unconscious voice of the resident is the best counsel we have. In order for the structure of a healing center to become viable, there must be an attitude of trust in each person's capacity and potential for wholeness. The staff should be present to nurture, facilitate, and release the whole-making energy in each individual.

. . . *to watch the play and dance of water in a fountain, to listen to it rush over stone, can be truly curative; it can inspire us and lighten the emotional timbre of the whole organism.*

VI

THE HEALING CENTER

The basic concept of the healing center is familiar in that it will consist of a complex of physical structures on land set apart from the normal activity of urban society. It will differ rather immediately in that greater use will be made of the land itself for its therapeutic and healing properties, and in that the architecture of the physical structures and the interior design will in many cases be drastically different from the rectangular buildings we are used to seeing.

As we move deeper into the realm of the invisible, we see that much of what we have accepted as part of our environment in the past needs to be re-examined in light of its effect on our consciousness. The rectangle and the square, for instance, are not necessarily healthful structures to live in. For the person simply living out his daily life, this may not be an important consideration. But in a healing center, where we are bringing about a change of consciousness and using every aspect of the life situation to accomplish this, the *shape* of the space we create will be vital.

The geodesic dome in the healing center suggests many uses. It may function as a kind of dwelling, or as a "work" area, where individual and group therapy may be conducted. Left open and furnished with plant life, the dome makes an ideal meditation center or "body space" for t'ai chi, yoga, and dance. It would no doubt be a very pleasant space for baths, saunas, and massage. The dome is so flexible that it will undoubtedly serve a hundred purposes.

The healing center should be a place where artists and architects can explore and experiment with space and shape. Especially in a place which is designed to return us to a sense of divinity, harmony and beauty, we must allow the creative soul to exercise imagination. We must break out of the narrow confines, the rectangles and squares which we have taken for granted for so many centuries.

Psychic Discoveries mentions that a hospital in Canada is using the trapezoid structure in working with schizophrenia, and recording success with this unusual space. No matter how unusual, as long as a structure has a postitive and beneficial effect, it is serving its highest function, for it then becomes part of the healing process.

The pyramid should be considered as a possible structure for the communal dining hall, not only because of the pyramid's effect on food, but also because of its effect on our perception of food.

This is important since one of the central aspects of the healing center will be the food that is served. Many people who come to the center will be suffering from the wrong diet . . . meat, sugar, chemicalized, refined and processed foods. Though this food makes them ill, they will be accustomed to it, and some may find it hard to change their way of eating. In order to help them make the transition to a natural and organic diet the pyramid will be invaluable.

The actual construction of geometric spaces for healing requires careful research. The incredible pyramid, for example, is rendered useless unless it is oriented to true north. The materials which are used will also be important. Ultraviolet transmitting plastic should be used where glass might normally be used, particularly near urban sites, where the majority of residents coming to the center will be suffering from a general lack of sunlight, and may be deficient in the ultraviolet ray of the spectrum. The pyramid structure covered with ultraviolet transmitting plastic could be used as a greenhouse where residents would combine a variety of healing elements including growing food.

Another way in which geometric structure can be used is in symbolic work. The use of these symbols would be particularly fruitful in work with insanity, for madness is largely a state which speaks in the language of symbol, myth, and archetype. Like the buildings in which the residents of healing centers dwell, work, and play, these symbols will serve to remind people of other states of being, and stir in them memories of wholeness.

One of the essential aspects of healing centers is that they be places which are designed to remind people of their inherent divine nature and of the whole-making, harmonious nature of the universe. Even if we had conclusive proof that meditation on certain symbols is healing, it is doubtful that a person entering a healing center in a particularly unbalanced state is going to have the energy or focus required to meditate. But if the resident could spend long periods of time in rooms designed with these symbols in mind, it is likely that these structures will do for him what he cannot do for himself—they will transmit healing energy to him.

Residents who have spent long periods of time undergoing therapy without any significant progress may need to have the will awakened. The will to be well must be present, for without it all therapies and all medicines lose their power. This awakening of will is the *decision* that Gurdjieff speaks of. Since that decision is related to the triangle, all therapy sessions for such a resident might be carried out in spaces where the triangle is significantly present. Here again the pyramid is useful, as is the geodesic dome. In a relaxed state, and at regular intervals, the resident might be asked to view images of geometric figures which contain the triangle. (This approach could of course be used with any of the geometric symbols.) If the therapist can have the resident repeat a simple mantra while viewing the triangle images, such as, "I will be well," or "I am strengthening my willpower," the effect will be deepened rapidly.

Since the square is the symbol of solidity and permanance, a resident who has difficulty in getting thoughts organized and bringing them to fruition might benefit by actually building something out of square panels or square stones. Involvement with the weight of the objects will further help to impress the meaning of the square in the resident's mind.

If the pentagram brings a sense of strength to the resident, the therapist might introduce, at the proper time, old situations which have in the past caused awkwardness in the resident. Let her speak to those situations from the physical position of the pentagram, out of a sense of wholeness and dominion.

The ideas above are all suggested as therapeutic *aids*. The use of geometric symbols is meant to underscore and facilitate the central theme of the therapeutic approach.

Earlier we looked at the various elements and their application to improve the "normal world" and the people who function in it on a day-to-day basis. In the healing center these vital components of good health should be intensified and adapted to suit the comfort and need of the residents. It is clear from what we have learned about negative and positive ions that healing centers should be set in beautiful, remote, rural areas where the air is clean and alive with energy. They will be areas where there is constant exposure to nature and the sense of meaning which nature instills in the mind and body.

How can the elements be used in the healing center? The first answer that comes to mind is they must be integrated into the activity of the healing environment. The way in which a resident spends time in a healing center will be determined by individual needs, by the demands of the process that he or she must undergo in order to complete the inner journey.

So let us speak of rest and activity, and the balance between them. The healing center must be a place in which complete rest is possible—deep rest—for there is much that can heal itself if given time and space to heal. There must be a sense of shedding, for awhile, the cares, the burden of life in the world, the external complexities, so that all energy is focused on the internal healing process. Everything here must be simplified. In ancient Greece this transition from external to internal work was ritualized in the aesclapias—retreats where people in crisis could go. (See Chapter on Dreams: Center and Soul.) Upon entering an aesclapia a person would shed his own clothes, be bathed and then given new clothes which were worn for the duration of the stay. A process like this might be undergone in the healing center. We must return to the original sense of the word asylum—a place of refuge and rest, where time and space is given to mend body, mind, spirit, emotion.

The other side of this scale is activity. There is very little to do in our institutions as they are presently structured. There are meals, and sometimes there is television. Other recreational activities depend greatly on the monetary status of the institution. The presence of television seems contrary to the work which must be done in healing people. At present, television is a clear reflection of the violence and meaningless activity which spawns the illness in our society. It nourishes the confusion and sense of emptiness that brings on emotional crisis and mental breakdowns. It is too infused with trivia, and triviality is in itself a kind of death-destruction process. I do not mean to disparage television totally. It is an incredible media, and its potential for exciting and valuable contributions to our culture is immense, but until it is consistently used in creative ways, it can have no place in healing centers. As it presently exists in hospitals and institutions, it is another kind of drug.

We must provide for the residents of healing centers

real activity—physical expression, creative expression, mental and emotional exercise, release, and stimulation. Such therapeutic, creative activity can include a wide range of possibilities. It is only important to keep in mind that in a healing center everything is taken into account—whatever is there, whatever is offered, must be considered a kind of nourishment. We must know what needs to be nourished and supported in the individual, and what food best supplies those needs. All must be balanced, aligned, and integrated.

In working with those who have come to the healing center because of emotional problems plant life should be considered a tremendously important support system. I have faith in the therapeutic process, in the miracle that can happen between two people really listening and speaking to one another. But in most cases it takes time, a long time, for such a relationship to have meaning and effect—time for the therapist to find a way to reach the resident, time for the resident to trust enough to let himself be reached. During this interim every means must be used to gently speak to, touch and open the resident. I know of no gentler, subtler beings than the plant life with which we share this earth.

A natural relationship with plant life, and a place in which the resident can be provided with meaningful contact with air, earth and water will be in gardens where vegetables, herbs and flowers are grown. For some, creative work with earth, using art as therapy to sculpt or work with clay and pottery, will provide great emotional release. Staff members who are artists and craftspeople will help inspire and guide such activity.

Since healing centers will employ these natural healing methods, residents will be exposed to a kind of life in which great quantities of time will be spent in fresh, clean air. Pleasant open-air spaces should be provided for people to exercise and move in, and these spaces must be designed for this kind of activity so that people feel comfortable and right moving in them. In this area I see staff being a reflection of fruitful living. If there are people present who are involved in body awareness, in the joy of being in a strong, healthy and beautiful body—people who are willing and glad to share their physical disciplines—then there is a greater possibility that residents will have an idea, or image of what it can be like to live like this, feel like this. People are also a part of environment and staff should consist of people who can provide healthy models for residents.

Physical disciplines such as yoga and t'ai chi ch'uan are excellent. Both use air to change and strengthen all the vital functions. Instruction should be available in these disciplines for those residents who need or are drawn to them, and for those who want to learn how to meditate, concentrate or simply how to breathe.

Centers will encompass a lifestyle in which movement is easy. The land and the buildings of the center will make it pleasant to walk, run, play outdoor games and be involved in outdoor exercise. There will be people present who know, and can instruct others, in different body awareness techniques. These will be shared with everyone who wants to learn and participate. The energy systems which support the center, such as large gardens that grow food for the center, will involve manual labor. Simple tasks such as raking leaves and hauling firewood will be part of the healing process for residents and staff. (Whoever thought to automate leaf-raking by inventing those large, noisy vacuums for people who keep grounds did a great dis-service to everyone. Not only do these machines diminish the health-giving aspects of this activity by reducing the movement involved to a bare minimum, they also turn the pleasant sound of leaves crackling together into a manufactured machine sound that only increases sound pollution and generally causes people to tighten up—defending their sensibilities against the noise. This is just another example of our strange notion that automation and convenience always "make life better" when in fact they often make life much worse.)

In speaking of energy systems that support the center, it occurs to me that it would be wise to have on the staff a person (or persons) whose specialization is energy: energy sources and ways of transforming and utilizing energy. At a time when we are at last beginning to see that we must both conserve and recycle the energy resources of this planet, we are also beginning to look to the sun. Here is our ultimate source of energy. The healing center should have someone on the staff who knows how to construct solar energy collectors, and the basic mechanics of constructing solar heating units.

The energy consultant should also understand the basics of electricity—its uses and limitations—steam power, windmills, and the mechanics of reconverting engines to cleaner energy sources.

Recycling is probably part of this job. The healing center should utilize everything possible. Like old tribes of the past, we must waste nothing.

Fire is another element which can be used in the healing process; since it can be an extremely dangerous and destructive element, its use as a healing agent must be carefully considered and controlled. When it is not possible to use it actually, it might be used in work with depth images, where it can transform without danger of physical harm.

The presence of fireplaces would, of course, be ideal. When one can watch firelight and feel its warmth it is restful to the mind and tends to heal the emotions. Fire is also important as ritual. Such acts as tending lamps, lighting candles, may well be included in ritual activity in healing centers.

Of all fire images, the sun itself is the most powerful and this image should be used in symbolic work. Activity in the sunlight should be encouraged. Sunbaths as well as walking and exercising in the sunlight should be a daily activity.

The use of water in the healing center has many possibilities. Pure water to drink is of tremendous importance, but its value does not stop there. Baths should be an integral part of the daily life in the center. Whoever is involved with water therapy should become familiar with cold water and its use as a healing agent.

A pool where residents can swim, play and exercise as well as steam baths and saunas should be included. A plentitude of meditative pools and ponds would help provide the healing effects of contemplation. The presence of aquariums and fountains would be soothing and inspiring.

In addition to the other benefits realized through activities involving the elements a natural derivative will be in the procurement of nourishing food. Whenever possible, a good deal of space should be provided for gardens. Diet at the center should be simple, consisting of grains, fresh fruits and vegetables, sprouts, dairy foods, beans, yogurt, nuts, seeds, organic juices and herbal teas. It is important that all the energy around food, the growing, harvesting, preparing and sharing should be surrounded with love. Whenever possible, it would be a good idea to plant and tend fruit trees and fruit bearing bushes. Staff should be available to tend these gardens and to teach and help residents who need and want to partake in this particular kind of activity. Gardening will be especially beneficial for those who are in transition from life in a healing center to life in the world again, since it is a change from a situation in which the resident is dependent to one in which she is depended upon.

For clinics or small centers where it is not possible to grow food, an independent source system should be arranged to obtain food from organic growers or natural food stores. However, healing centers should provide as much natural food for the community as possible.

In adjusting to a different and healthful diet, the most important things the center will provide are time and supportive space. It will certainly provide complete information and, in a direct and experiential way, an alternative way of life. It will also provide a complex educational system as to how to function in and be a part of this alternative, because living in a center is the process by which you learn how to live differently. It is in providing time and an alternative, supportive space that I see the healing center playing a tremendous role in effecting positive change.

This supportive space is necessary to make changes in one's own life. In terms of food, when everything that is available to you is healthful, it will be easy to eat in a healthful way. When other people around you fast regularly, it is not so much effort to fast yourself. A day of silence observed by an entire community makes silence simple. When people are given, or give themselves, supportive space, change is not only possible, it is natural.

The people who staff healing centers will need to be familiar with natural remedies, to be in touch with the laws of simple and intelligent diet, pure water, fresh air, sunlight, and a balance of rest and exercise. The herbalist and naturopath will be vitally important to the staff of a healing center. There will be no need for drugs or chemicals in the healing center, for it is a place where we will leave behind artificial methods, mechanicalness, and the sterility that accompanies it.

Color will be important in all aspects of the healing center and the color specialist a valuable member of the staff. The person who works in this area will be one who knows in all its subtle details the therapeutic value of colors and could recommend a "color prescription" which would help to bring the whole organism back into a balanced state. Special consideration should also be given to color in the rooms where staff members meet to make decicions. These rooms should be color designed to aid clarity and empathy.

I can also foresee a color treatment center, which will be a building in which people receive individual and specific color treatment, by taking "color baths." A possible design for such a center would probably make use of the circle as a basic floor plan. It would then be easier to facilitate use of the "zodiacal master plan" of color healing. The geodesic dome might be ideal for such a building.

One possible design for such a color treatment center would be a basic circular floor quartered by a cross. These four paths would be entranceways to the center of the building. The paths would be more like arbors, made graceful and alive with plant life. A meditative pool of water, perhaps a lotus pool or a fish pond, would be located in the very center of the building. Around this pool the area would be, basically, a lounge and administration center, where residents could sit, and staff would be available to help and direct residents to the color treatment rooms. Each of these rooms would have a small transition room between the lounge and the color treatment area, where residents might strip or change into loose clothing. The color treatment room would be one in which residents could lie or sit comfortably, and be immersed in a particular color, made luminous by natural light. When natural light is not available with the kind of intensity necessary, artificial light would be available. It would be interesting to explore the use of hydrogen light for this purpose, because of its bright and luminous quality. The whole design of the building should be one which enhances a receptive state in those who are to receive color treatment. Arbored entranceways, a meditative pool, a quiet, comfortable lounge, and privacy in the color treatment rooms will all help to induce a receptive state.

Healing centers should be located in areas where noise, the constant input of unnatural sound, is left behind. The rhythm and natural music of the countryside will help to heal the senses, and make space in the resident to hear the wisdom of the inner Self. Opening this "inner ear" requires that a certain degree of stillness be present. We must allow time and space for this transition to stillness to occur in the resident, and be sensitive to what the individual needs, to that which will enable him to experience a measure of peace.

Silence—true silence—is an important medium in which this transition can occur. Twice I have slept in a room which was entirely built of concrete, had absolutely no windows, but did have a good ventilation system. I thought that I would be frightened in such an atmosphere, because it was tomb-like. Once I had gone inside the room and turned out the light, it was pitch black and there was no sound, no trace of the outside world. (I need to add that sleeping in this room was entirely voluntary and that the lock on the door was inside. There was no sense of being imprisoned or of *having* to stay in the room.) After the first night there I woke feeling incredibly peaceful and deeply rested. This experience was repeated upon sleeping there again several nights later. I felt safe in this room and, even more important, external stimuli were completely removed. In the total silence and darkness, my senses were able to rest to a degree which is not often possible.

I would like to see such rooms (which I think of as "silence chambers") available in healing centers. Their use must be wisely administered, for no one must feel forced to stay in such absolute isolation, and there are cases where such a room might disturb or frighten a resident. But for others this opportunity to shut out the world will be welcomed, and for these residents the kind of deep rest possible in such a room will hasten the healing process and help bring about a state of receptivity to other therapy.

Another mode of experiencing stillness and silence is in meditation. The healing center should provide space for people to meditate, and staff who can help and instruct residents in different methods of meditation, postures, and whatever might be needed to make the benefits of meditation available to residents. When, where, and if meditation is prescribed will be dependent on the individual. For some it may be important to include meditation as a daily therapeutic exercise almost immediately. For others it may not be useful or possible until other changes have occurred.

Every healing center should have a library. In it one would find a selection of books which pertain to the life of the community—books on health, on organic gardening, on herbs, on light and color, and on the various therapeutic methods used at the center. On these shelves books on spiritual and psychic healing would be readily available, as well as books concerning various spiritual paths and disciplines. There would be a plentitude of works by authors who inspire the inner life and work on the self. The staff should feel welcome to contribute a list of books which they have found personally helpful. (Not necessarily helpful in therapeutic techniques, but in terms of feeling more alive, of having captured meaning and essence.) Books on hypnosis and self-hypnosis, dreams, prayer, and the power of thought and image should all be available.

The library would, in short, be a collection of healthful books. For those residents who want to read, there should be a wide selection of books which can instruct them about health and healing methods, and connect them with both positive and powerful voices. Roberto Assagioli, in speaking of developing the will, recommends appropriate reading to provide inspiration and encourage perseverance. This recommendation applies to developing any quality. The right book gives us a framework, puts us within a certain mood, influences our thought forms and often enables us to find the necessary strength and discipline to change.

In addition to books, the complete library should have a selection of music, and of images. Photographs, reduced prints, and slides are all ways of making images available. I am thinking particularly of images which are evocative of the dream state, of fantasy and fairy tale—images in which we visually experience archetypes, and which awaken inner perception.

The music library, in addition to having tapes and records, will also house the musical instruments which belong to the community. I cannot imagine the healing center without music, for it will be a place where people sing and dance together. Especially in creating rituals, and for people involved in movement and dance within the community, the availability of simple musical instruments will be important.

The complete healing center will most certainly involve people in the performing arts, and those who are in touch with the power of theatre to move us to deepened and expanded perception of ourselves and of our world. Centers should make use of psychodrama, the acting out of dreams, dance and mime, and ritualized encounters and celebrations. The staff should include persons who dramatize and satirize the members and the life of the community. The actors and dancers, the clowns and magicians, the musicians and those who create theatrical settings, will be there to move us to tears and laughter, reveal us to ourselves, and perhaps release and open avenues which we did not know were possible, or had forgotten. The theatre is very powerful and much needed in understanding and working with the soul. It is work in which we need the artist.

Several years ago Anais Nin said, "In our time the world is chilled by mind and by analysis."[45] Our parents built institutions based on mind, on analysis, on a belief in science, rationality, and technology. We who conceive and design the healing centers of the future are in need of the artist more than the analyst. The artist, who is in love with beauty, who is committed to mystery, who is always seeking to express essence and soul through material mediums, is a central figure in this mandala of creating wholeness. We suffer the indignities of people concerned with function. The artist (and the true craftsman) always seeks a way to weld function and beauty, to integrate the practical and the external with the aesthetic needs which are within us. While the analyst is concerned with examining and separating (a necessary part of the creative process), the artist extends the examination to fusion, to synthesis.

In a world too dominated by the materialist's concern to expose everything, to make all the facts known, we need the poet, who loves what is hidden, who pursues the gossamer secrets of essence beneath and behind what is tangible. In the realm of theatre this pursuit has a natural environment. It is because of this that I hope artists will always find a welcome place in the healing center, for they are so much a part of the healing process.

It is my hope that every healing center will also have someone skilled in the practice of hypnosis and its use in therapy, change and expansion; and that those who are ready and show interest will have guidance and help in developing self-hypnosis skills. The results which are possible with hypnosis and self-hypnosis are truly incredible. People who are involved with healing centers and who will be most in need of learning about, and having access to, information about image, affirmation, suggestion and self-hypnosis are those who are directly concerned with creating healing centers, and residents who are leaving centers to return to the world. In both these situations, people will be faced with a great deal of problem solving, and should have ready access to the wonderful resources of the subconscious mind, wherein are all solutions.

Dreams will also be an important part of the healing

center and work with them will have a central role in the life of the community. I see dreams interwoven into daily activity in a very direct way, and the center treating them as the Senoi do—with an approach that entails respect, understanding and pragmatism.

One possible stumbling block to this natural inclusion of dreams in the healing center is that certain residents may be unfamiliar with work on dreams, and may have an attitude that dreams are not important. It is only recently that growth psychology has taken dream work out of the private sanctuary of the high priests of the unconscious (the analyst and the therapist) and given them back to people. It would not surprise me to find that many people are still out of touch with their dreams or still consider them something that only "experts" should deal with. If this is the case, the resident should certainly not be forced to change her attitude, nor should her attitude disrupt the philosophy and processes of the center. There are certainly a myriad of alternatives available for working with such a resident, and it may be that the experience of the healing center will, in time, bring about a natural change in the way the resident views dreams, and his own dream life.

For residents who have an interest in the occult sciences, alternative methods should be available. We have discussed the use of color therapy earlier. A color therapist should work closely with other diagnosticians to indicate which colors are needed to bring the system back into balance.

Although I do not see residents being given "readings" by palmists, chirognomy can be a valuable psychological tool where individuals of depth who are skilled in this art are available. Actual contact between the resident and the palmist should be minimized, only allowing as much as the palmist feels is needed to give his psychic sense of the person time to operate. Much of the diagnosis will take place in the privacy of the palmist's own study or office, where prints or photographs of the hands can be studied at leisure. From this an analysis of the resident can be presented to the staff members.

A biorhythm chart for each resident would be of tremendous value. This is a method which is becoming openly accepted even in guiding ones abilities and periods of decision-making in the business world. It would certainly be of value in indicating which periods during the residence of an individual would be most rewarding for certain aspects of therapy.

If we give a resident a Tarot deck and ask her to choose what is meaningful, and then to create some kind of a narrative about why these images are meaningful, we will undoubtedly discover much of what the resident needs in therapy, as well as what is needed in symbolic healing. To a resident who is leaving the center to begin life anew the talents of a numerologist may be of special help.

Most people are probably more familiar with astrology than any of the other occult sciences and of course this could be a useful tool initially as used in diagnosis, for treatment, and to aid the resident who is adapting herself to leaving the center.

Although we have explored many approaches to healing physical, mental and emotional disturbances, the whole of this complex therapy can be reduced to just two vital ingredients: nutrition and prayer. By nutrition I mean that we must pay attention to what needs to be nourished, and how to nourish those needs. Though people who come to the center have a variety of ills and complaints, the main condition will be one of depletion in one form or another. It is because of this that the underlying attitude of the staff members in healing centers is very important. There must be a basic sense of love and respect in the atmosphere, strength and patience which radiates from staff members, a benign attitude that includes faith and the expectation of health.

To create such an atmosphere implies much about the inner resources and spiritual character of staff members. I am not referring to moral character. Morals are mostly a social adjunct and change with the character and climate of the society. Spiritual character has much more to do with the essence of a person, with clarity of consciousness, with intention, and with the simple but profound degree of love which is present.

Work in a healing center will be incredibly challenging and demanding. There must be a realistic appraisal of what can be expected from a staff member. Especially in the sensitive area of channeling and transferring energy directly, care must be taken among the staff to renew themselves and periodically clarify their own aura.

In addition to the general atmosphere created in the healing center, certain periods should be set aside each day for concentrated psychic healing work. All the staff members in a healing center should be able to participate in such psychic healing sessions. Psychic healing may not be the medium in which all staff members feel most alive or able to help, and I do not mean to imply that everyone *should* participate in these sessions. There will undoubtedly be a group of people who feel their most effective work takes place in these meditative sessions, and they will be the ones who make psychic healing a regular part of the daily rhythm in the center. But these sessions should be open to all staff members and residents. The spiritual strength and inspiration which can be gained from participating in a session of psychic healing will benefit not only the individuals concerned, but the whole timbre and quality of life in the community.

VII.

TRANSITION SPACE

Since the healing center will be a very different environment and way of life for most people, especially people who live in cities, a transition space, or halfway house, should be established for people who are going to become residents of a center for any length of time. These transition places should also serve those who are leaving centers after a length of time, in order to cushion the culture shock of returning to the "world." In planning for those who are either going to healing centers or leaving them, those who administer and organize centers should remember two watch-words from t'ai chi ch'uan: go slowly, and gently.

Going

The transition house will be found once removed from the city, in out-lying areas or small towns, on residential streets where the noise of traffic is diminished or seldom heard, where there are lawns, trees, backyard gardens, and the peaceful hum of human activity in comfortable settings. They will be large houses, set up cooperatively, and I imagine they will eventually be staffed by people who are former residents of healing centers and wish to remain associated with the center. Since they will have experienced the center, they will be in an ideal position to help those who are going.

As with the healing center, length of stay in the transition house will vary. I imagine that the shortest period of time will be spent by those who are physically well and are going to the center for a period of retreat, in order to rest or contemplate major and critical changes in their lives. The longest stay will be for those who are ill and have been taking medicine in the form of drugs. For these people, a de-toxification period will be necessary. As Jethro Kloss has stated so clearly, drugs and herbs do not mix. Drugs introduce into the system an externalized chemistry which activates the system quickly. Herbs and natural healing methods work through a process of allowing the internal chemistry of the body to function as it was designed to—perfectly and harmoniously. Because the healing process begins from within, it does not ncessarily produce results as quickly as using drugs. But the results are long-lasting and they do no harm. They last as long as you are willing to follow simple rules of preventative medicine. There are no side effects, or deaths caused by "the medicine" as there are with drugs.

Food will probably be the major change for most people. I see these transition houses set up very much like Doctor Ann Wigmore's healing houses in Boston, or the clinics and sanitoriums in Europe. People will basically be resting and changing their diet. There should be ample, competent help from people who understand fasting, and nutrition.

Time in a transition house may also be used to review and state clearly to oneself why one is going to a healing center, and to make a serious commitment to the process of self-healing.

Leaving

As the picture of the healing center becomes more and more complete, the inevitable question arises: "Why would you want to leave?" Why, indeed? The center provides beautiful structures on spacious land, organic foods in plentiful quantity, freedom to choose one's work and contribution to the community, and to abide by one's own rhythm, a supportive, intelligent and creative society of people to dwell with, rituals designed to nourish and guide the spiritual quest so inherent in the human animal, the most evolved methods of health care, and the possibility of expansion through the free sharing of knowledge. This is a utopia which it is difficult to imagine people wanting to leave.

Many people who have listened to me talk about the healing center have asked about this. It seems unlikely that people suffering from the distress, pollution, and injustices of our present environment, healed by an ideal environment, will want to return to the world.

But as with any situation, different people are going to do different things, make different choices. It is very likely that some people, having once experienced the healing center, will choose to spend several months—or even years—within the green retreat of the center. It is just as likely that some people will never leave at all. If, as the Braginskys have shown, people can make a reasonable adaptation to the depressing environment of the mental institution and live a more meaningful life within its confines than they could on the "outside," it seems reasonable to conclude that some people will prefer the healing environment to life in the world and will stay there. These people will, in time, become an active part of the community, taking on the work that must be done in any gathering of human beings, helping others—in a way which suits their abilities and temperament—to make the inner journey one undergoes in a healing center.

However, it is unrealistic to assume that everyone will want to stay in the center simply because everything will be provided for them. Variety is the keynote in creation, and change is the only constant. Not everyone will want the way of the retreat, which is essentially what the center is. Some will need, or want, the challenge of returning to the world.

Many residents will have left friends and family, children or parents behind. With the restoration of mental and physical health and with a new knowledge of what life can be, they may want to return to their loved ones to share their new wisdom.

Though the transition may be a very difficult one, especially for long-term residents of healing centers, for some it will be a necessary transition. Just as some people will inevitably stay, some will inevitably feel called to go back to the world and help change the conditions which took them to the center in the first place. I am not saying that this dedication to change is inevitable, or that it will be the main motivation of people leaving the healing center. But my intuition tells me that people who find their own center again by being within the center, who grasp an expanded sense of themselves because of the healing environment, and who are humanized by being dealt with humanly, will feel a sense of kinship with the rest of the human race still suffering the ignominious existence of an ignorant civilization. They will want to help, to affect changes, to guide others, to make an impact on a society which induces a sense of powerlessness. I think the good sense, kindness, and feeling which pervades an old saying of the American Indian—"With all beings we shall be as relatives"—will be a natural result of one's stay in a healing center.

For those who are leaving the center, the transition house will provide a place to acclimate to a more normal pace of living, to renew gradual contact with the world, and to begin undertaking responsibilities. Much of this "renewal of responsibility" will be through helping to staff the transition house, providing help and guidance for those who are going to the center. The transition house will also be a place where communication with the community can begin again, especially for those who are interested in devoting their time to endeavors which will help to make the world environment a healing environment.

PART FOUR

BEGINNING

IMAGE

I am tossing this book
like a stone
into the water
watching the circles
healing
circles
ripple
extend
expand
expansion
into
always
joining other
circles
born
of
other stones
and the
flow
of love
grows.

I

THE PRAYER OF THE AGNOSTIC, THE DREAM OF THE FAITHFUL

Not long ago I saw a film by Ingmar Bergman called *Cries and Whispers.* I was most moved, stirred in the very foundation of my being, by the prayer of the Chaplain, as he says the final words over the dead body of Agnes. It is the prayer of the agnostic. It is the very essence and heart of doubt.

> If it is so that you have gathered our suffering in your poor body, if it is so that you have borne it with you through death, if it is so that you meet God over there in the other land, if it is so that He turns His face toward you, if it is so that you can then speak the language that this God understands, if it is so that you can then speak to this God—if it is so, pray for us. Agnes, my dear little child, listen to what I am now telling you. . . . Lay your burden of suffering at the God's feet and ask Him to pardon us. Ask Him to free us at last from our anxieties, our weariness, and our profound doubt. Ask Him for a meaning to our lives. Pray for us who are left here on the dark, dirty earth, under an empty and cruel Heaven.[46]

Later that night I had a dream. I remember only images of circles and pentacles, and a voice which gave me these messages: Seek your solutions in corresponding elements. If you have a question about earth, there is an answer in earth. If you have a question in life, there is an answer in life.

The dream seemed a clear reverberation caused by the impact of doubt. The Chaplain in me asked, "Is there any meaning to all this?" And my soul replied clearly, "Yes." In Colin Wilson's book, *The Occult*, he states repeatedly that it is a sense of meaning which puts us in touch with our limitless potential, and sparks the will to action. Once we have recognized meaning, nothing is beyond us. It is in moments of stillness, of inner quiet, that we can catch this translucent meaning—the radiant pattern of a harmonious universe is just beneath and below our normal, everyday, rush-about consciousness.

> Suddenly and miraculously, as you walk home in the dark, you are aware of the insubstantial shimmering essence that lies within appearances, the air is filled with expectancy, alive with meaning; the stranger, gliding by in the lamplit street, carries silently past you in the night the whole mystery of his life . . .[47]

The reality of our present environment and the work at hand is admittedly staggering. There is so much and so many to be healed. War is a constant theme—the din of battle and the threat of violence is always either present or hovering in some corner of the world. The dual effects of over-population and pollution threaten our very existence. There are still so many people committed only to personal power and aggrandisement. There are still so many struggling with personal survival, who do not have the energy to give to recreating a beautiful earth. The prophecies of doom could become a reality, unless we act intelligently, completely, and quickly. For those of us who can see, who have the capacity to effect change, it is time—it is past time—to begin. Every single person is a center of consciousness and will. Because of this every single person is capable of changing the environment—the total environment. But we must act now.

> We have a deeply ingrained habit of passivity
> which is more dangerous than cigarette smoking or
> drugs . . . man needs to develop an automatic sys-
> tem for dealing with these poisons that arise from
> stagnation, from the endless triviality of civilized
> life . . . He must develop the "mental muscle" I
> have spoken of: Faculty X. . . . The next stage in
> human evolution will be the deliberate develop-
> ment of this "muscle" of the will, and a correspond-
> ing development in the sense of meaning.[48]

We can change the world. To do this we must become
aware of the dark, external reality. And at the same time
we must contact our own divinity, which is within, and
become the gods and goddesses which we truly are. We
must awaken to the inner reality, our potential, wherein
we can find the wisdom, strength, and will to transform
our lives, and the earth.

II

GATHERING TOGETHER

When I began researching environmental healing, I lived in a community of people who were well versed in natural healing and growth psychology. There was a general air of acceptance, and these past few years I have watched a steady rise in the number of people who are beginning to doubt orthodox medicine and turn more to holistic healing. I have no way of knowing about you, the reader, or to what degree the material of this book is familiar—or unfamiliar—to you. My hope is that I have elucidated my vision of the healing environment so clearly that all of you, both initiates and old disciples of natural healing, will want to begin the work of building healing centers.

This book presents a great deal of research, and I care that the evidence I give you be strong, clear, and that it have a reliable source. But my deepest concern is to move you, the reader, to act. I do not really believe that a presentation of facts alone is enough to move anyone, nor do I think it necessary to make my evidence for an alternative overly meticulous. If you have eyes to see and ears to hear, if you move through the mainstream of this country, you know as well as I that we cannot for long tolerate our present hospitals, institutions, prisons, poverty, and ghettos. Every person in this country who is ill, starving, homeless, abused, forgotten, or is lacking in the basic needs of all human beings is in some way a part of us. If we do not soon gather the energy to heal ourselves, if we do not begin soon to heal the environment, then the weight of the illness will draw the rest into misery. The strong must help the weak, until they can help themselves.

I am not putting forth a case for welfare. I am talking about compassion and intelligence. Out of simple compassion, and basic intelligence, those of us who can, must help to bring about change. For in change lies our salvation.

Beginning

During a recent seminar on hypnosis the instructor brought in a biofeedback mechanism which let you know the quality of your thoughts by a sound that it made. If your thoughts were generally positive and peaceful, it made a gentle, humming sound. If your thoughts were worrisome, agitated, or negative, it made a static sound. We decided to try an experiment with this mechanism. We linked hands, and each of us attempted to put ourselves into a meditative state, to see if we could establish a peaceful current between us. The experiment was working quite well, when another member of the seminar came into the room. We explained what we were doing, and she joined us. Rather quickly, the machine started to make the static noise, and continued to make it even though we stayed with it for awhile. When we checked with each member of the group, it turned out that the newcomer had had a very trying day. All the while that she was participating in the experiment, she had doubted her ability to achieve a quiescent state.

This story is significant because most people do not carry around such a biofeedback mechanism, and I think it is very important to remember, in any undertaking, that the kind and quality of each person's thought and energy matters. The creation of healing centers is a big job, and it will take a great deal of conscious, loving, and enlightened energy to accomplish it. I would like to talk a little about possible ways to begin, and things to watch for along the way.

The first step is, of course, to begin with yourself, by finding out in what ways you can make your own living harmonious with the principles of a healing environment. On a larger scale, if there are groups of people involved in natural healing in your area, contact them. Find out who they are, what they're into, how you feel about them, how they feel about you. If it feels right, discuss with them possible ways in which a healing center, or clinic, can be created. If there is no group like this in your area, or at least not one that you feel comfortable with, you will have to begin one. I stress your feeling right with the group because I think healing centers, though built on the same principles, will vary with the personalities who join together to build them. Many different kinds of people will be interested and it is only natural to gravitate toward people who have a somewhat similar lifestyle. You should feel comfortable together.

Given that there is no group already operative, talk to your friends, family, and neighbors about these ideas. See how many people in your area are dissatisfied with our present mental institutions and traditional medicine. Gather together with these people and share your feelings about what is and what can be. Share your personal views about possible alternatives. If you know legislators who might think the healing center is a possibility, talk to them. If you know people who are professionals in the mental health field or doctors who are sympathetic to natural healing methods, contact them and ask them to join you. The help of such people is invaluable.

I think one natural outcome of gatherings such as these will be the sharing of natural healing principles and experiences. Although this is important, especially in the beginning, do not let yourselves get too distracted by this kind of activity. Unless your main reason for getting together is to share experiences and knowledge, circumscribe that activity. If your principal reason for getting together is to start a center or a clinic, it will take a great deal more than just talking about it.

It will also be important to find one person, or a group of people, who can give all or most of their time to providing leadership for the total group. Too many people with good intentions and fine plans become fragmented and finally fall apart because there is no adequate leadership. There has to be someone, or a handful of people, who have the time, strength, and ability to organize, direct, focus, and keep vital the energy of the group. They must have their lives worked out in some way so that they can financially afford the time it will take to give such leadership. This leadership must, of course, have the approval and acceptance of the group.

Don't start out by making too many compromises. Get a clear idea of what you want, and then start asking how you can manifest this. Once you have a group of people and are ready to begin, spend a day together in a comfortable, quiet setting—and dream. Remove all limitations. Pretend you have direct, ready access to the richest bank in the universe, and give yourself permission to create the kind of healing center you really want. What feels right for your particular area, and this group of people? Once you dream your mutual dream, you can begin figuring out how to actualize the dream. Apply the principles of imaging what you want and affirming its reality.

One warning: Just as there are people interested in health and healing, there are people who are invested in illness, some of them unconsciously so; but there are those who are actively invested in warfare, poverty (or rather their own aggrandizement), and racial and class struggles. It is quite possible that these people will oppose the establishing of healing centers, for the nature of the healing center is such that people who leave them will find it hard to tolerate the status quo, and will have a natural commitment to expanding the healing environment. Those who need to defend the status quo may fear those who want to change it, and will oppose them. I regret that this is so, but it has to be dealt with. The lessons of Watergate and other matters which have recently come to light, are in themselves a warning against naivete. However, it is good to remember the advice of the *I Ching* in this area, which is: don't give too much attention or energy to your opponent. Don't get trapped in the enemy game, or give too much thought to your own faults or failings. Instead, concentrate on the good in yourself, in others, and on the good that can be done. If you find one door locked, don't spend too much time pounding at it. Try another route.

People who start centers and clinics will initially be involved in finding suitable space (buildings and land), locating funds to acquire that space, or finding people who have space and are willing to contribute it to this kind of alternative. Suitable environments must then be created, or available environments modified to meet the requirements of the center. Next, there must be funds to staff and maintain these centers, and people who can administer them properly. When you get that far, I hope this book is just one of many on the shelves of the healing center that will help you the rest of the way.

At this point of beginning, I'd like to paraphrase something which Tolstoy said a long time ago: If evil people can join together to get what they want, so can good people join together to get what they want. It's so simple.

III.

AN ACT OF FAITH

The healing center is not only the Aquarian alternative to the Piscean institution. It is potentially a powerful agent for change. We can begin to nourish, on multitudinal levels, the life-giving values which ultimately are our only salvation from the self-destruction which our present society is proliferating. This book is for every single individual who has recognized the need for change. It is for all those who value life above profit. It is for those who are compassionate and humane in spite of the deadening forces of our technological age, and who are optimistic in spite of our present world situation.

It is all these people I hope to reach in presenting a vision and an outline of how we can heal ourselves and the environment. The work of healing is truly a Magnum Opus—a great work—in every sense of the word. It is the only work which truly matters. Even if your work is not directly involved with healing or growth psychology, it is possible to live your life and make your work harmonious with the principles of the healing environment. And it is possible to contribute time and energy to making the healing environment a reality. It is going to take all of us to do this. The earth is our home. I cannot see how people can consider themselves separate from the task of healing our home, unless they have serious plans to escape in a spaceship to some better place.

It is not too late. We can change; we can fashion a better world. We must have faith, not only in our own potential, but in the harmonious, health-oriented life force which is invisible yet constantly tangible, and which can help us if only we will let it. As an act of faith, let those of us who care gather together, pool our resources, unify our energy, and begin.

NOTES

1. Steve McNamara, "Learning to Use Both Halves of Your Brain," *Pacific Sun* (week of April 4–10, 1974), p. 10.
2. Jethro Kloss, *Back to Eden* (fourth edition, Riverside: Lifeline Books, 1972, 1973), p. 109.
3. Roberto Assagioli, *Psychosynthesis* (New York: Hobbs, Dorman & Company, Inc., 1965), p. 193.
4. S. G. J. Ouseley, *The Power of the Rays* (London: L. N. Fowler & Co., Ltd., 1951), p. 9.
5. Kloss, op. cit., p. 11.
6. Joan Grant, *Winged Pharoah* (New York: Berkeley Publishing Corporation, 1969) p. 22.
7. Sheila Ostrander and Lynn Schroeder, *Psychic Discoveries Behind the Iron Curtain* (Englewood Cliffs: Prentice-Hall, Inc. 1971), p. 201.
8. Ibid. p. 204.
9. Grant, op. cit., p. 23.
10. Corinne Heline, *Color and Music in the New Age* (Oceanside: New Age Press, Inc., 1969), p. 38.
11. Ostrander, op. cit., p. 370.
12. Pyrameditation Brochure (Fresno, California).
13. P. D. Ouspensky, *In Search of the Miraculous* (New York: Harcourt Brace & World, Inc., 1949), p. 281.
14. Loc. cit.
15. Ibid., p. 282.
16. Loc. cit.
17. Assagioli, op. cit., P. 258.
18. Richard Wilhelm, tr., *The I Ching*, English tr., Cary F. Baynes (third edition, Princeton: Princeton University Press, 1969) pp. 68, 69.
19. John N. Ott, *Health and Light* (Old Greenwich: The Devin-Adair Company, 1973), p. 47.
20. Ibid., p. 48.
21. Mike Samuels and Hal Bennett, *The Well Body Book* (New York and Berkeley: Random House Bookworks, 1973), p. 98.
22. George Downing, *The Massage Book* (New York and Berkeley: Random House Bookworks, 1972), p. 1.
23. Harry Lorayne and Jerry Lucas, *The Memory Book* (New York: Ballantine Books, 1974), p. 17.
24. Teilhard de Chardin, *The Phenomenon of Man* (second edition, New York: Harper & Row, Publishers, 1965), pp. 283–285.
25. Fred Gettings, *The Book of the Hand* (London: The Hamlyn Publishing Group Limited, 1971), pp. 23, 25.

26. Ibid., p. 16.
27. Ann Faraday, *Dream Power* (New York: Berkeley Publishing Corporation, 1973), p. 269.
28. Suevo Brookin, lecture given at *An Herbalist Retreat* (Laney Ranch, Occidental, California, May 20th, 21st, 1975).
29. D. L. Rosenhan, "On Being Sane in Insane Places," *Science* (January 19, 1973), p. 179.
30. Benjamin M. Braginsky and Dorothea D. Braginsky, "Mental Hospitals as Resorts", *Psychology Today* (March 1973), pp. 22, 24.
31. Rosenhan, op. cit., p. 179.
32. Anais Nin, *The Novel of the Future* (New York: Collier Books, 1970), pp. 61, 62.
33. Rosenhan, op. cit., p. 251.
34. Braginsky, op. cit., p. 24.
35. Ibid., p. 31.
36. Rosenhan, op. cit., pp. 178, 179.
37. Ibid., p. 257.
38. Braginsky, op. cit., p. 24.
39. Ibid., p. 32.
40. Assagioli, op. cit., p. 193.
41. Buckminster R. Fuller, *Operating Manual for Spaceship Earth* (New York: Pocket Books, 1971), p. 79.
42. Brookin, op. cit.
43. Jane Roberts, *The Nature of Personal Reality* (Englewood Cliffs: Prentice-Hall, Inc., 1974), pp. 387, 388, 389.
44. Erich Fromm, *The Art of Loving* (New York: Harper & Row, Publishers, 1956), p. 110.
45. Anais, Nin, *The Diary of Anais Nin*, 1934–1939, ed. Gunther Stuhlmann (New York: The Swallow Press and Harcourt Brace and World, Inc., 1967), p. 80.
46. Ingmar Bergman, "Cries and Whispers," *The New Yorker* (October 21, 1972), p. 45. Order of sentences in this quote is rearranged to be in keeping with dialogue as it appeared in film production.
47. Alan McGlashan, *The Savage and Beautiful Country* (Boston: Houghton Mifflin Company, 1967), p. 157.
48. Colin Wilson, *The Occult* (New York: Random House, 1971), pp. 565, 566, 569.

BIBLIOGRAPHY

Adams, Paul, *The New Self-Hypnosis*. North Hollywood: Wilshire Book Company, 1973.

Airola, Paavo O., *Health Secrets from Europe*. West Nyack: Arco, 1970.

Amber, R. B., *Color Therapy*. Calcutta: Firma K. L. Mukhopadhyay, 1964.

Assagioli, Roberto, *Psychosynthesis*. New York: Hobbs, Dorman & Company, Inc., 1965. 323 pp.

Bates, W. H., *The Bates Method for Better Eyesight Without Glasses*. New York: Pyramid Books, 1974.

Bennett, Samuel, *Be Well*. New York and Berkeley: Random House Bookworks, 1974.

Bergman, Ingmar. "Cries and Whispers," *The New Yorker* (October 21, 1972), Pp. 38–74.

Besant, Annie, and, Leadbeater, C. W. *Thought Forms*. Wheaton: The Theosophical Publishing House, 1969. 77 pp.

Bugental, J. F. T., *The Search for Authenticity*. New York: Holt, Rinehart and Winston, Inc., 1963. 437 pp.

Capote, Truman, *The Grass Harp and A Tree of Night*. New York: Signet Books, 1945.

Carter, Mildred, *Helping Yourself with Foot Reflexology*. West Nyack: Parker Publishing, 1969.

Case, Paul Foster, *The Tarot*. Richmond: Macoy Publishing Company, 1947. 214 pp.

Clark, Barbara, *Body Proportion Needs Depth*. Urbana: Barbara Clark, 1975.

Clark, Linda, and Yvonne Maritime. *Health, Youth and Beauty Through Color Breathing*. Millbrae: Celestial Arts, 1976.

Da Liu, *T'ai Chi Ch'uan and I Ching*. New York: Harper and Row, Publishers, 1972.

de Baïracli-Levy, Juliette, *Nature's Children: A Guide to Organic Foods and Herbal Remedies for Children*. New York: Warner Paperback Library, 1972.

de Baïracli-Levy, *Common Herbs for Natural Health*. New York: Schocken Books, 1974.

de Chardin, Teilhard. *The Phenomenon of Man*. Second edition, New York: Harper & Row, Publishers, 1965. 320 pp.

Dintenfass, Julius, *Chiropractic: A Modern Way to Health*. New York: Pyramid Publications, 1970.

Downing, George, *The Massage Book*. New York and Berkeley: Random House Bookworks, 1972.

Faraday, Ann, *Dream Power*. New York: Berkeley Publishing Corporation, 1972.

Frank, J., *Persuasion and Healing*. Baltimore: John Hopkins Press, 1961.

Fromm, Erich. *The Art of Loving*. New York: Harper & Brothers Publishers, 1956. 133 pp.

Fromm, Erich, *The Forgotten Language: An Introduction to the Understanding of Dreams, Fairytales and Myths*. New York: Holt, Rinehart and Winston, 1951, 1970.

Fuller, R. Buckminster. *Operating Manual for Spaceship Earth*. New York: Pocket Books, 1971. 127 pp.

Garten, M. O., *The Health Secrets of a Naturopathic Doctor*. New York: Lancer Books, Inc., 1967.

Gettings, Fred, *The Book of the Hand*. London: The Hamlyn Publishing Group Limited, 1971. 213 pp.

Goodman, Morris C., *Modern Numerology*. North Hollywood: Wilshire Book Company, 1970.

Grant, Joan, *Winged Pharoah*. New York: Berkeley Publishing Corporation, 1969. 310 pp.

Hall, Manly Palmer, *Healing, The Divine Art*. Los Angeles: Philosophical Research Center, 1944, 1971.

Hall, Manly P., *Studies in Dream Symbolism*. Los Angeles: The Philosophical Research Society, Inc., 1965.

Heline, Corinne. *Color and Music in the New Age*. Oceanside: New Age Press, Inc., 1969. 117 pp.

Hunter, Beatric Trum, *Food Additives and Your Health*. New Canaan: Keats Publishing, Inc., 1972.

Jung, C. G., *Memories, Dreams, Reflections*. New York: Pantheon Books, 1963.

Kerrell, Bill, and Goggin, Kathy, *The Guide to Pyramid Energy*. Santa Monica: Pyramid Power-V, Inc., 1975.

Khan, Hazrat Inayat, *The Sufi Message of Hazrat Inayat Khan: Volume IV, Health*. London: Sufi Publishing Co., Ltd., 1974; orig. pub. London: Barrie and Rockliff, 1962.

Khan, Sufi Inayat, *Music*. New Delhi: The Sufi Publishing Co., 1973; orig. pub. London: Barrie & Rockliffe, 1962.

Kloss, Jethro, *Back to Eden*. New York: Beneficial Books, 1972. 671 pp.

Kriyananda, *Yoga Postures for Self-Awareness*. San Francisco: Hansa Publications, 1967.

Lappé, Frances Moore, *Diet for a Small Planet*. New York: Ballantine Books, 1975.

Le Cron, L., *Techniques of Hypno-Therapy*. New York: The Julian Press, 1961.

Lerza, Catherine, and Jacobson, Michael, eds. *Food for People, Not for Profit*. New York: Ballantine Books, 1975.

Lopez, Vincent, *Numerology*. New York: The Citadel Press, 1967.

Lorayne, Harry, and Lucas, Jerry, *The Memory Book*. New York: Ballantine Books, 1975.

Lucas, Richard, *Nature's Medicines.* New York: Award Books, Universal Publishing and Distributing Corporation, 1969.

Lust, John, *The Herb Book.* New York: Bantam Books, 1974.

Maltz, Maxwell, *Psycho-Cybernetics.* North Hollywood: Wilshire Book Company, 1969.

Man-ch'ing, Cheng, and Smith, Robert W., *T'ai Chi: The "Supreme Ultimate" Exercise for Health, Sport, and Self-Defense.* Rutland: Charles E. Tuttle Co., 1967.

Maslow, Abraham H., *Toward a Psychology of Being.* New York: Van Nostrand Reinhold Company, 1968. 240 pp.

McGlashan, Alan. *The Savage and Beautiful Country.* Boston: Houghton Mifflin Company, 1967. 157 pp.

McLuhan, T. C., *Touch the Earth.* New York: Pocket Books, 1972. 185 pp.

McNamara, Steve, "Learning to Use Both Halves of Your Brain," *Pacific Sun* (week of April 4–10, 1974). P. 10.

McQuire, Thomas, *The Tooth Trip.* New York and Berkeley: Random House Bookworks, 1972.

Medical Group, Theosophical Research Centre, *The Mystery of Healing.* Wheaton: The Theosophical Publishing House, 1958, revised edition, 1968.

Murphy, Joseph, *The Power of Your Subconscious Mind.* Englewood Cliffs: Prentice-Hall, Inc., 1963.

Nin, Anais. *The Diary of Anais Nin, 1934–1939.* ed. Gunther Stuhlmann, New York: The Swallow Press and Harcourt, Brace & World, Inc., 1967. 357 pp.

Ostrander, Sheila, and Schroeder, Lynn. *Psychic Discoveries Behind the Iron Curtain.* Englewood Cliffs: Prentice-Hall, Inc., 1971. 457 pp.

Ott, John N., *Health and Light: The Effects of Natural and Artificial Light on Man and Other Living Things.* Old Greenwich: The Devin-Adair Company, 1973.

Ousby, William J., *Self-Hypnosis and Scientific Self-Suggestion.* New York: Arc Books, 1966.

Ouseley, S. G. J., *The Power of the Rays.* London: L. N. Fowler & Co., Ltd., 1951.

Ouspensky, P. D. *In Search of the Miraculous.* New York: Harcourt, Brace & World, Inc., 1949. 399 pp.

Oyle, Irving, *The Healing Mind.* Millbrae: Celestial Arts, 1975.

Pelikan, Wilhelm, *The Secrets of Metals,* tr. Charlotte Lebensart. Spring Valley: Anthroposophic Press, Inc., 1973.

Perry, John. "The Creative Element in Madness" (mimeographed).

Ramacharaka, *The Science of Psychic Healing.* London: L. Fowler, 1960.

Roberts, Jane, *The Nature of Personal Reality: A Seth Book.* Englewood Cliffs: Prentice-Hall, Inc., 1974.

Roberts, Jane, *Seth Speaks.* New York: Bantam Books, 1972.

Rosanes-Berrett, Marilyn, *Do You Really Need Glasses?* New York: Hart Publishing Company, 1974.

Rosenhan, D. L., "On Being Sane in Insane Places," *Science*, Volume 179, January 19, 1973. Pp. 250–257.

Samuels, Mike, and Bennett, Hal, *The Well Body Book*. New York and Berkeley: Random House Bookworks, 1973.

Serizawa, Katsusuke, *Massage: The Oriental Method*. Tokyo and San Francisco: Japan Publications, Inc., 1972.

Szekely, Edmond Bordeaux, *The Essene Gospel of Peace*. San Diego: Academy of Creative Living, 1971.

Szekely, Edmond, *Medicine Tomorrow: Introduction to Cosmotherapy with Guide to Treatment*. Ashingdon: C. W. Daniel Company, Ltd., 1957.

Taylor, Renee, *Hunza Health Secrets for Long Life and Happiness*. Englewood Cliffs: Prentice-Hall, Inc., 1964.

Thommen, George. *Biorhythm*. New York: Award Books, 1969. 157 pp.

Tompkins, Peter, and Bird, Christopher, *The Secret Life of Plants*. New York: Harper and Row, Publishers, 1973.

Turner, Gordon, *An Outline of Spiritual Healing*. New York: Warner Paperback Library, 1972.

Vithaldas, *The Yoga System of Health and Relief from Tension*. New York: Cornerstone Library Publications, 1957.

Warmbrand, Max, *The Encyclopedia of Health and Nutrition*. New York: Pyramid Books, 1974.

Waters, Frank, *The Book of the Hopi*. New York: Ballantine Books, Inc., 1972. 423 pp.

Weed, Joseph J., *Wisdom of the Mystic Masters*. West Nyack: Parker Publishing Company, Inc., 1968. 208 pp.

Weiner, Michael A., *Earth Medicine-Earth Foods*. New York: Collier Books, 1972.

Wigmore, Ann, *Be Your Own Doctor*. St. Paul: Dan Pilla Printing and Engraving.

Wilhelm, Richard, tr., *The I Ching*. Third edition, Princeton: Princeton University Press, 1969. 740 pp.

Wilson, Colin, *The Occult*. New York: Random House, 1971. 601 pp.

Index

BOOKS OF RELATED INTEREST

TIME, SPACE AND THE MIND by Dr. Irving Oyle explores the mind's incredible ability to switch off time/space as the single most powerful healing tool available to humanity. 128 pages, soft cover, $4.95

Stanley Krippner and Alberto Villoldo's REALMS OF HEALING presents a scientific exploration of non-medical healing and healers around the world, with emphasis on current laboratory research in the USA, the USSR, Brazil and Canada. 252 pages, soft cover, $6.95

In MAGIC, MYSTICISM AND MODERN MEDICINE, Dr. Irving Oyle paints engrossing, staccato scenarios of his experiences as director of an experimental health service doing research in holistic healing. 128 pages, soft cover, $3.95

THE COMPLETE BOOK OF ACUPUNCTURE by Dr. Stephen Thomas Chang provides basic philosophy and practical applications of acupuncture for both laymen and physicians. Introduction by Dolph B. Ornstein 252 pages, soft cover, $6.95

Penetrating chapters on pleasure, freedom, fear, death, time, the unconscious mind, love, sexuality, meditation, and human evolution make THE PASSIONATE MIND by Joel Kramer an important manual for contemporary living. 128 pages, soft cover, $3.95

THE PAIN GAME by internationally known neurosurgeon C. Norman Shealy teaches the reader to break the chronic pain habit through a technique of balancing the body's physiology to achieve emotional attunement. 156 pages, soft cover, $4.95

THE HEALING MIND, controversial, disturbing, fascinating first book by noted lecturer and medical researcher Dr. Irving Oyle, describes what is known about the mysterious ability of the mind to heal the body. 128 pages, soft cover, $4.95

CELESTIAL ARTS
Millbrae, California

$4.95

Healing Ourselves With and Through the Environment

earth energy • color therapy and the human aura • structural design
geometric symbol • sound and silence • light and life • compassion
mitment, and consciousness • the occult sciences as diagnostic tool
spiritual and psychic healing • dreams as soul food

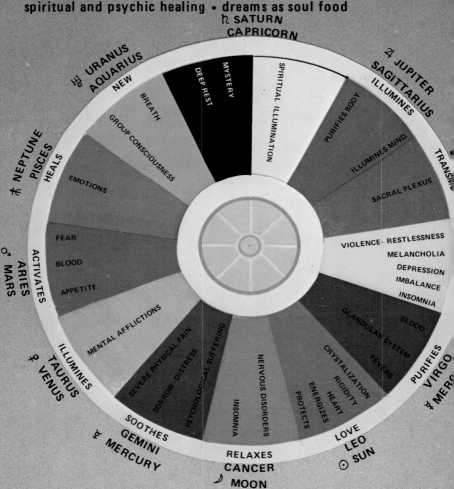

The Healing Environment... *touches one humanly and clarifies t
which would be less effective told in an abstract way as ideas. I l
and I believe every word....You arouse many speculations, rever
and the desire to act. ...*

Anaïs Nin

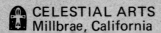

CELESTIAL ARTS
Millbrae, California

ISBN: 0-89087-021